First published in 2008 by True Publishing
Chaworth Road
West Bridgford
Nottingham
NG2 7AB

Text © 2008 Katie Crookston
Photographs © 2008 Katie Crookston
Design and Layout © 2008 Matt Trueman & Sally Trueman

www.DairyFreeCakeRecipes.co.uk

ISBN 978-0-9560413-0-2

Printed in China

Dairy and Egg Free Cake Recipes

Katie Crookston

For Grandma

Contents

Introduction

How it all started...

My parents first realised that my brothers, sisters and I were allergic to dairy and egg products when I was about five years old. Fortunately for us our grandma was a professional baker. She started to experiment with cake recipes which she could make for us to take to school for lunch and enjoy at the weekends. Over the years my grandma developed a whole range of recipes for cakes, biscuits, slices, breads and puddings many of which we still enjoy as a family today.

The cakes she made were so delicious and far tastier than my memories of bought cakes from the supermarket, it was then I became interested in baking. She taught both my sisters and I how to bake and ever since she passed away I have carried on the tradition of baking cakes for the family and creating new recipes for us all to enjoy.

My family and the long list of food allergies...

Some members of my family are not only allergic to eggs and dairy products, but to soya, citrus fruits, grapes, apples and dates as well. We have all grown up in a constant battle to correctly identify the cause of what seemed to be ever new reactions.

It is amazing when you start looking at product ingredients to discover just how many foods have one or more of the above, therefore through experimentation I have now discovered substitutes for nearly all of these so I can make cakes and puddings the whole family can enjoy.

About the Dairy and Egg Free Cake Recipe Book

I am sure any parent will agree that discovering your children have certain food allergies can be a very confusing, daunting and frustrating time. Once an allergy is diagnosed a whole set of new challenges arise largely centred around how to give your children a 'normal' diet without limiting their options.

This recipe book has been written to hopefully help those parents and children who may have now grown up and have their own families to shortcut the 20 years of trial and error I have had. Everyone can now make great tasting dairy and egg free cakes to share and enjoy for all occasions from afternoon tea or Sunday lunch to birthdays and Christmas.

Notes on Ingredients

Dairy Substitutes

Non-dairy sunflower margarine can be used instead of butter or a margarine that contains dairy products. I use Pure Sunflower margarine which works well with all the recipes in this book.

The Pure brand was developed for people with food sensitivities in mind, particularly those who have an allergy or intolerance to dairy. It was launched into health food stores in the early 1990s, and is now widely available in all retailers throughout the UK and Ireland.

Pure is free from:

- Dairy
- Gluten
- Artificial colourings, preservatives & flavourings
- Hydrogenated oils
- Genetically modified ingredients

Pure spreads are suitable for use in all forms of cooking and baking, and taste great making them suitable for the whole family. There are three varieties; Pure Soya, Pure Sunflower, and Pure Organic.

For more information visit www.puredairyfree.co.uk

There are several alternatives to cow's milk now available in the shops. I use soya milk in my recipes which is currently available as fresh, long life and long life organic. It has added vitamins and minerals including more calcium than is in most cows' milk so makes an excellent alternative.

If you are also allergic to soya milk as well as cow's milk as my sister is, you can use rice milk as a substitute, which can also be found in most supermarkets. Rice milk is a good non-dairy alternative which is also sugar free. Some rice milks are also enriched with calcium to make them equivalent to the levels found in cows' milk. Both these types of milk can be used in all the recipes in this book.

As additional alternatives, you can also use coconut milk or even lactose free milks, all will work fine.

Fruit and Nut Substitutes

There are several recipes in this book which contain dried fruits, nuts or both. In case of any allergies to these or if you have any particular preferences, here are some alternatives which you may find useful:

Instead of walnuts, you can use pecan nuts. They are both similar in texture and flavour.

Instead of currents, raisins or sultanas, you can use dried sour cherries or cranberries. As my mum is allergic to vine fruits they have made an excellent substitute for her.

Instead of raisins or sultanas, you can use dates or apricots.

Instead of mixed peel you can use chopped dried pineapple. Similarly you can use pineapple juice instead of orange juice or lemon juice if you are allergic to citrus fruits.

All of these alternatives can be used in any of the relevant recipes you find in this book.

Dry Ingredients

Some icing sugar products surprisingly contain egg. 'Royal Icing Sugar' will always contain eggs so steer clear of this. Others icing sugars may contain traces of egg so it is always worth reading the product information before purchasing them.

I use dark chocolate which has at least 70% cocoa content instead of milk chocolate. Please take care when buying dark chocolate as I have found some brands contain lactose which is a dairy product.

I normally use dark muscovado sugar instead of dark soft brown sugar as I find it improves the flavour of the finished cakes.

Freshly grated nutmeg has a lot more flavour than ready ground nutmeg and will make your cakes taste better.

I find 'Easy to use' yeast gives more consistent results than fresh yeast because sometimes the dough doesn't rise very well due to the 'fresh' yeast not being fresh enough.

If you don't have any caster sugar in your cupboard you can use granulated sugar as a good substitute.

Be sure to read the ingredients on everything you buy to make sure they do not contain any dairy or egg products.

Before using this Book...

Tips

Use non-stick unbleached baking parchment instead of greaseproof paper if you can find it. If not, normal baking parchment will do just as well. I find it better to use than greaseproof paper as it can be removed from the cake more easily once the cake has cooked and it doesn't need any additional greasing to make it non-stick.

I sift all the flours, icing sugar and cocoa powder before they are mixed with the rest of the ingredients. This ensures all the lumps are removed and therefore they will combine better with the rest of the mixture. Sifting the flour also ensures plenty of air is added into the cake mixture which is very important for dairy and egg free baking as it helps the cake to rise.

Notes

Each 'Recipe Facts' section provides a guide as to whether each recipe contains dairy, eggs, nuts, gluten, soya and wheat. Whilst I have tried to ensure this is as accurate as possible it is the reader's responsibility to review recipe ingredients and product ingredients to avoid adverse reactions.

Please note the cooking times given in these recipes are ones which work with my oven and may vary slightly with your oven. Take care not to overcook and check until you become more familiar with the recipes and how they work with your oven.

Each 'Recipe Facts' guide states whether the resulting cake is suitable for freezing. Where freezing is possible, the cake should be cooled to room temperature, wrapped in tinfoil and if available put into either a freezer bag or suitable container, and then placed in the freezer.

The following abbreviations have been used throughout the recipes in this book; tsp = teaspoon, tbsp = tablespoon, g = grams, ml = millilitres.

Cakes

Squidgy Chocolate Cake

If you like chocolate you will really enjoy this cake recipe as it is made with 100g of melted dark chocolate. The soft sponge layers combined with the chocolate butter cream and gooey chocolate icing makes it so squidgy it is hard to pick up! This chocolate cake makes a great birthday cake or just a wonderfully indulgent treat.

Recipe Facts

Preparation Time: 40 minutes   Cooking Time: **15 minutes**

Dairy Free	Yes	**Gluten Free**	No
Egg Free	Yes	**Soya Free**	No
Nut Free	Yes	**Wheat Free**	No

Suitable for Freezing: **Yes**

Ingredients

100g dark chocolate, melted
90g non-dairy sunflower margarine
280g dark muscovado sugar
220ml soya milk
315g plain flour, sifted
2 tsp baking powder

For the chocolate butter cream:
155g non-dairy sunflower margarine
90g icing sugar, sifted
60g cocoa powder, sifted

For the chocolate icing:
125g icing sugar, sifted
60ml cold water (approx)
50g cocoa powder, sifted

Method

Grease two deep 20cm round sandwich tins and line with baking parchment.

Melt the chocolate and leave to cool to room temperature. Cream together the margarine and sugar in a large mixing bowl or food processor until light and fluffy, then add 3 tbsp of the milk and mix together. Don't worry if the mixture curdles slightly.

Add the melted chocolate and stir until smooth. Immediately add the rest of the milk and mix together.

Add the sifted flour and baking powder and blend the mixture in a food processor to make sure there are no lumps of flour. You may need to add a little extra milk to get your mixture to a dropping consistency i.e. the mixture slowly drops off your spoon.

Spoon the mixture into the prepared tins.

Bake in a moderate oven at 180°C (Conventional Electric Oven) for about 15-20 minutes until the cakes are just about coming away from the sides of the tins and when a skewer is placed into the centre of the cakes it comes out clean. Cool the cakes on a wire rack.

To make the chocolate butter cream, cream together the margarine and sugar in a small mixing bowl until light and fluffy. Add the sifted cocoa powder and stir until smooth and creamy.

To make the chocolate icing add icing sugar and a little water into a small bowl and stir until the icing sugar has dissolved. Then add the cocoa powder and stir until smooth and there are no lumps.

Once the cakes have cooled, sandwich together with chocolate butter cream and top with chocolate icing.

Banana Cake

This banana cake recipe makes a light, tasty and very moist cake which is even nice for breakfast! The tastier the banana's you use the better the cake so use well ripened bananas. As the filling has fresh bananas in it, it's best served as soon as the cake is made as the bananas will go brown over time.

Recipe Facts

Preparation Time: **40 minutes**   Cooking Time: **15 minutes**

Dairy Free	Yes	**Gluten Free**	No
Egg Free	Yes	**Soya Free**	No
Nut Free	Yes	**Wheat Free**	No

Suitable for Freezing: **No**

Ingredients

185g self-raising flour, sifted
½ tsp baking powder
155g granulated sugar
60g non-dairy sunflower margarine
185g ripe bananas
90ml (6 tbsp) soya milk
½ a whole nutmeg, grated

For the banana cream:
155g non-dairy sunflower margarine
90g icing sugar, sifted
185g bananas, chopped

Method

Grease two 18cm round sandwich tins and line with baking parchment.

Add the flour, baking powder, sugar and margarine into a large mixing bowl. Mix well until the mixture resembles fine breadcrumbs.

Mash the bananas with the milk and nutmeg in another mixing bowl. Add this to the dry ingredients and mix well.

Spoon the mixture into the prepared tins.

Bake in a moderate oven at 180°C (Conventional Electric Oven) for about 15-20 minutes, depending on your oven, until the mixture has just started to come away from the sides of the tins, and a skewer comes out clean when placed into the middle of the cakes.

Cool the cakes on a wire rack.

To make the banana cream add the margarine and sugar into a small mixing bowl and mix until smooth and creamy. Add the bananas and mix together.

Sandwich the cakes together once they have cooled with the banana cream, dust the top with icing sugar and serve.

Rich Cherry Chocolate Cake

This is a very chocolaty cake recipe, ideal for chocoholics.....two layers of rich sponge, held together with soft, chocolate butter cream and juicy black cherries, then topped with melted chocolate. It's extremely tasty, and keeps very well for a few days, but only if you can resist eating it!

Recipe Facts

Preparation Time: 40 minutes   Cooking Time: **15 minutes**

Dairy Free	Yes	**Gluten Free**	No
Egg Free	Yes	**Soya Free**	Yes
Nut Free	Yes	**Wheat Free**	No

Suitable for Freezing: **Yes**

Ingredients

125g non-dairy sunflower margarine
180ml cold water
2 tbsp cocoa powder, sifted
100g dark chocolate, chopped
220g granulated sugar
110g self-raising flour, sifted
75g plain flour, sifted
Large tin of pitted black cherries, halved

For the topping:
100g dark chocolate, melted

For the chocolate butter cream:
155g non-dairy sunflower margarine
90g icing sugar, sifted
60g cocoa powder, sifted

Method

Grease two deep 20cm round sandwich tins and line with baking parchment.

Into a medium sized saucepan, add the margarine, water, cocoa powder, chopped chocolate and sugar. Stir over a low heat until the sugar has dissolved then cool the mixture for about 10 minutes.

Stir in the sifted flours (both the self-raising and plain) until the mixture is smooth and there are no lumps of flour remaining. To remove any lumps of flour, blend the mixture in a food processor, electric blender or with a hand whisk.

Bake in a moderate oven at 180°C (Conventional Electric Oven), for about 15-20 minutes until the cakes are just about coming away from the sides of the tins and when a skewer is gently placed into the centre of the cakes it comes out clean.

Stand the cakes for 2-3 minutes before turning out onto a wire rack to cool.

To make the chocolate butter cream, cream together the margarine and sugar in a small mixing bowl until light and fluffy. Add the sifted cocoa powder and stir until smooth and creamy.

Sandwich the cakes together with a layer of chocolate butter cream and the black cherries.

Top cake with the melted chocolate and serve once the chocolate has set.

Note – the black cherries can easily be omitted if preferred.

Spicy Carrot Loaf

Spicy carrot loaf is an interesting variation on a traditional carrot cake. The cake is very moist as the fruit is boiled before being added into the cake mixture and it has an extra dimension added through the spices. It is well worth making and will keep for several days in an air tight container.

Recipe Facts

Preparation Time: 40 minutes   **Cooking Time: 45 minutes**

Dairy Free	Yes	**Gluten Free**	No
Egg Free	Yes	**Soya Free**	Yes
Nut Free	No	**Wheat Free**	No

Suitable for Freezing: Yes

Ingredients

135g carrot, grated
130g dried sour cherries, chopped
170ml water
165g granulated sugar
30g non-dairy sunflower margarine
1 tsp ground cinnamon
½ a whole nutmeg, grated
60g pecan nuts, chopped
110g self-raising flour, sifted
110g plain flour, sifted
½ tsp baking powder

Method

Grease a loaf tin (14cm by 21cm) and line the base and sides with baking parchment.

Mix together the carrot, cherries, water, sugar, margarine, cinnamon and nutmeg in a saucepan. Stir constantly over heat, without boiling, until the sugar is dissolved.

Bring to the boil then reduce the heat, cover and simmer for 10 minutes. Cool to room temperature.

Stir in the chopped nuts and mix thoroughly. Then add in the sifted flours and baking powder. Stir the mixture well until there are no lumps of flour remaining. Spoon the mixture into the prepared tin.

Bake in a moderately low oven at 160°C (Conventional Electric Oven) for about 45-50 minutes or until the cake has just started to come away from the sides of the tin.

Stand for about 5 minutes before turning onto a wire rack to cool.

Dark Sticky Ginger Cake

Ginger cake is always a family favourite, and this is no exception. The dark muscavado sugar and black treacle give it a lovely stickiness, while the cake itself remains quite light. The cake is delicious served warm with custard or eaten cold on its own. It keeps really well for a few days in an airtight container.

Recipe Facts

Preparation Time: 40 minutes   Cooking Time: **30 minutes**

Dairy Free	Yes	**Gluten Free**	No
Egg Free	Yes	**Soya Free**	No
Nut Free	Yes	**Wheat Free**	No

Suitable for Freezing: **Yes**

Ingredients

125g non-dairy sunflower margarine
150ml soya milk
2 tbsp golden syrup
2 tbsp black treacle
225g self-raising flour, sifted
115g dark muscovado sugar
1 tbsp ground ginger
1 tsp ground cinnamon

Method

Line a deep 20cm round cake tin with baking parchment.

Add the margarine, milk, syrup and treacle together into a saucepan. Heat until the margarine has melted and they have all combined together. Cool for about 10 minutes.

Add the flour, sugar and spices into a mixing bowl or food processor. Mix until combined.

Add the treacle mixture to the dry ingredients and mix thoroughly until smooth and there are no lumps of flour.

Pour the mixture into the prepared tin.

Bake in a moderate oven at 180°C (Conventional Electric Oven) for about 30-35 minutes or until the cake is starting to come away from the sides of the tin. Check the cake is cooked with a skewer, ensuring it comes out clean when gently placed into the centre of the cake.

Cool the cake in the tin.

Serve with custard or rum sauce (see section 'Sauces, Icings & Fillings') or just enjoy on its own.

Apple Cake

If you like apples, you will love this cake recipe, it has become my brother's favourite. This moist cake is lovely and soft, and scattered with pieces of apples, nicely contrasted with a crunchy, sticky topping. It tastes even better if it is made with home grown Bramley apples.

Recipe Facts

Preparation Time: 40 minutes   **Cooking Time: 50 minutes**

Dairy Free	Yes	**Gluten Free**	No
Egg Free	Yes	**Soya Free**	No
Nut Free	Yes	**Wheat Free**	No

Suitable for Freezing: **Yes**

Ingredients

125g non-dairy sunflower margarine
250g dark muscovado sugar
60ml (4 tbsp) soya milk
250g plain flour, sifted
½ whole nutmeg, grated
1½ tsp ground cinnamon
2 tsp baking powder
250g cooking apples, peeled, cored and chopped

For the topping:
2-3 tsp clear honey or golden syrup
1-2 tsp demerara sugar

Method

Grease a deep 7 inch round cake tin and line the sides and the bottom with baking parchment.

Cream together the margarine and sugar in a large bowl until light and fluffy then add in the milk. Do not worry if the mixture curdles a little at this point.

Stir in the flour, spices and baking powder. Use either a food processor or a blender to make sure the mixture is smooth and has no lumps in it.

Stir in the chopped apples. You may need to add a little extra milk if the mixture is not at a dropping consistency i.e. the mixture slowly drops off the spoon.

Spoon the mixture into the prepared tin.

Bake in a moderate oven at 180°C (Conventional Electric Oven) for about 50-55 minutes, until the cake has just started to come away from the sides of the tin and a skewer comes out clean when gently placed into the middle of the cake.

Turn the cake out on to a wire rack and cool.

Top the cake with a thin layer of honey or golden syrup and sprinkle with demerara sugar.

Spicy Golden Ginger Cake

Unusually for ginger cakes, this cake is not made from black treacle but golden syrup which gives the cake its golden brown colour. It is very light in texture and thanks to all the added spices, very tasty too. It is an easy cake to make and keeps very well for a few days in an airtight container.

Recipe Facts

Preparation Time: 30 minutes   Cooking Time: **25 minutes**

Dairy Free	Yes	**Gluten Free**	No
Egg Free	Yes	**Soya Free**	No
Nut Free	Yes	**Wheat Free**	No

Suitable for Freezing: **Yes**

Ingredients

125g non-dairy sunflower margarine
230ml golden syrup
220g granulated sugar
300g plain flour, sifted
1 tsp baking powder
1 tbsp ground ginger
1 tsp ground cinnamon
1 tsp ground mixed spice
85ml soya milk

Method

Grease a 20cm by 24cm slab cake tin and line it with baking parchment.

Add the margarine and syrup into a saucepan and stir over a low heat until the margarine has melted. Cool to room temperature.

Stir in the sugar, flour, baking powder, spices and milk. Use a food processor, a hand whisk or a blender to get the mixture to a smooth consistency.

Pour or spoon the mixture into the prepared tin.

Bake in a moderate oven at 180°C (Conventional Electric Oven) for about 25-30 minutes until the cake is just starting to come away from the sides of the tin and a skewer comes out clean when gently placed into the middle of the cake.

Turn the cake out onto a wire rack and leave to cool.

Simple Jam Sponge

This sponge cake is a very simple cake to make as the name suggests. It uses basic ingredients with the option of putting any jam of your choice in the middle. It makes a perfect alternative to a traditional Victoria sponge cake and is just as good, making it an ideal birthday cake for all ages.

Recipe Facts

Preparation Time: 30 minutes   Cooking Time: **15 minutes**

Dairy Free	Yes	**Gluten Free**	No
Egg Free	Yes	**Soya Free**	No
Nut Free	Yes	**Wheat Free**	No

Suitable for Freezing: **Yes**

Ingredients

185g non-dairy sunflower margarine
185g granulated sugar
105ml (7 tbsp) soya milk
375g self-raising flour, sifted
Strawberry jam

For the butter cream:
155g non-dairy sunflower margarine
90g icing sugar, sifted

For the plain white icing:
200g icing sugar, sifted
30ml water (approx)

Method

Grease two deep 20cm round sandwich tins and line with baking parchment.

Cream together the margarine and sugar in a large mixing bowl until light and fluffy.

Add the milk and mix well. You can use a blender, food processor or a hand whisk to mix in the milk and ensure plenty of air is added into the mixture.

Add the flour and mix well, making sure you get all the lumps out of the mixture and it is a smooth dropping consistency i.e. the mixture slowly drops off the spoon. To get it to the right consistency you can use a food processor, hand whisk or a blender.

Spoon the mixture into the prepared tins.

Bake in a moderate oven at 180°C (Conventional Electric Oven) for 15-20 minutes until lightly golden and the cakes have just started to come away from the sides of the tins. Also check with a skewer, ensure it comes out clean when placed gently into the middle of the cakes.

Turn the cakes out onto a wire rack to cool.

To make the plain white icing add the icing sugar and a little water into a small bowl and stir until the icing sugar has dissolved and it's the right consistency to spread.

To make the butter cream add the margarine and sugar into a small bowl and mix until smooth and creamy.

Sandwich the cakes together with a thick layer of strawberry jam and the plain butter cream, then spread the top of the cake with the plain white icing.

Butterfly Cakes

These butterfly cakes are an easy and fun variation on the coconut sponge cake recipe. Delicious filled with jam and butter cream but they can also be finished with icing and glacé cherries to make an ideal children's lunchbox treat.

Recipe Facts

Preparation Time: 30 minutes   **Cooking Time: 15 minutes**

Dairy Free	Yes		**Gluten Free**	No
Egg Free	Yes		**Soya Free**	No
Nut Free	Yes		**Wheat Free**	No

Suitable for Freezing: **Yes**

Ingredients

125g non-dairy sunflower margarine
220g granulated sugar
150ml (10 tbsp) soya milk
45g desiccated coconut
300g self-raising flour, sifted
Strawberry jam

For the butter cream:
155g non-dairy sunflower margarine
90g icing sugar, sifted

Method

Place 24 paper cake cases into two 12 hole bun tins.

Cream together the margarine and sugar in a large mixing bowl until light and fluffy.

Add the milk and mix well. Use a blender, food processor or a hand whisk to mix in the milk and ensure plenty of air is added into the mixture.

Add the coconut and mix well.

Add the flour and mix well, making sure there are no lumps in the mixture and it is a smooth dropping consistency i.e. the mixture slowly drops off the spoon. To get it to the right consistency you can use a food processor, a hand whisk or a blender.

Spoon the mixture into the prepared paper cake cases.

Bake in a moderate oven at 180°C (Conventional Electric Oven) for 15-20 minutes until lightly golden. Check with a skewer, ensure it comes out clean when placed gently into the middle of the cakes.

To make the butter cream add the margarine and sugar into a small bowl and mix until smooth and creamy.

Once the cakes have cooled, cut a hole in each one and add about half a teaspoon of strawberry jam and a teaspoon of plain butter cream.

Place the cut out piece of cake on top to make it look like a butterfly.

Coconut Sponge Cake

This twist on a sponge cake recipe is quick to make and cook. The flavour of the cake can be altered slightly by adding pineapple juice instead of orange juice if preferred. The coconut works really well in the sponge, giving it extra texture and flavour. This coconut sponge cake makes a great birthday cake for all ages.

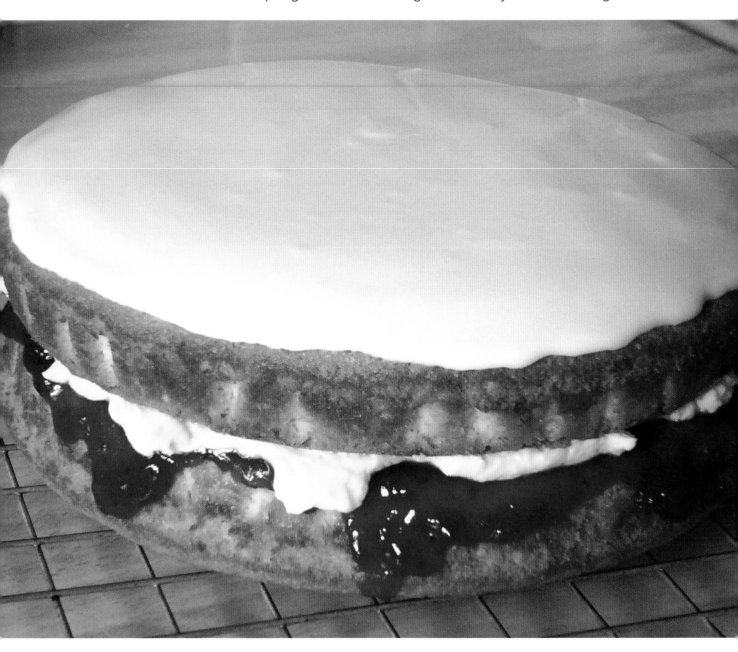

Recipe Facts

Preparation Time: 30 minutes   Cooking Time: **15 minutes**

Dairy Free	Yes	**Gluten Free**	No
Egg Free	Yes	**Soya Free**	No
Nut Free	Yes	**Wheat Free**	No

Suitable for Freezing: **Yes**

Ingredients

125g non-dairy sunflower margarine
Grated rind of 2 lemons
220g granulated sugar
45ml (3 tbsp) soya milk
45g desiccated coconut
300g self-raising flour, sifted
125ml orange or pineapple juice

For the plain white icing:
200g icing sugar, sifted
30ml water (approx)

For the butter cream:
155g non-dairy sunflower margarine
90g icing sugar, sifted

Method

Grease two deep 20cm round sandwich tins and line the bases with baking parchment.

Cream together the margarine, rind and sugar in a food processor or a large mixing bowl until light and fluffy. Stir in the milk but don't worry if the mixture curdles slightly, then stir in the desiccated coconut.

Alternately add flour and fruit juice, stirring after each addition until you have a dropping consistency i.e. the mixture slowly drops off the spoon. You may need to add a little more or less juice than specified to get it to the correct consistency. Once this is reached, spoon the mixture equally into the prepared tins.

Bake in a moderate oven at 180°C (Conventional Electric Oven) for about 15–20 minutes, depending on your oven, until lightly golden brown and the cakes are just coming away from the sides of the tins. Check with a skewer, ensure it comes away clean when placed into the centre of the cakes. Then cool on a wire rack.

To make the white icing add icing sugar and a little water into a small bowl and stir until the icing sugar has dissolved and it's the right consistency to spread.

To make the butter cream add the margarine and sugar into a small bowl and mix until smooth and creamy.

Sandwich the cake, once cooled, with a thick layer of strawberry jam (or any jam you choose) and plain butter cream. Then spread with plain white icing.

Variation

Follow the recipe above and add 60g of dried cherries or raisins to the mixture, after you have added all the other ingredients. Spoon the mixture into paper cake cases and cook as above. Mini fruit cakes!

Date and Nut Loaf

This loaf is really nice served warm and spread with some non-dairy sunflower margarine but is also wonderfully tasty without. The dates and walnuts combine excellently together adding fruit and crunch to this soft, crumbly and very moreish loaf.

Recipe Facts

Preparation Time: **30 minutes**   Cooking Time: **50 minutes**

Dairy Free	Yes	**Gluten Free**	No
Egg Free	Yes	**Soya Free**	No
Nut Free	No	**Wheat Free**	No

Suitable for Freezing: **Yes**

Ingredients

250g plain flour, sifted
2 tsp baking powder
125g granulated sugar
125g non-dairy sunflower margarine
45ml (3 tbsp) soya milk
30g walnuts, chopped
30g pecan nuts, chopped
250g dried dates, chopped

Method

Grease a 13cm by 23cm loaf tin and line with baking parchment.

Add the flour, baking powder and sugar into a large mixing bowl and mix well. Then add in the margarine and rub in until the mixture is crumbly.

Add the milk and mix well. Then stir in the nuts and dates.

Spoon the mixture into the prepared tin.

Bake in a moderate oven at 180°C (Conventional Electric Oven) for about 50 minutes to an hour until golden brown and it has just started to come away from the sides of the tin. Check with a skewer, ensure it comes out clean when placed into the middle of the cake.

Cool on a wire rack.

Slice the loaf and spread with margarine or enjoy on its own.

Sultana Cakes

This is a simple, plain, old fashioned recipe which my Grandma used to bake. When fresh, these cakes crumble into your mouth. Soft, juicy sultanas pop into each mouthful adding fruity flavour and texture to these simple, tasty bites. They are very easy to make and quick to cook.

Recipe Facts

Preparation Time: 20 minutes   Cooking Time: **8 minutes**

Dairy Free	Yes		**Gluten Free**	No
Egg Free	Yes		**Soya Free**	No
Nut Free	Yes		**Wheat Free**	No

Suitable for Freezing: **Yes**

Ingredients

250g self-raising flour, sifted
90g granulated sugar
90g non-dairy sunflower margarine
90g sultanas
45-60ml (3-4 tbsp) soya milk

Method

Line an oven tray with baking parchment.

Add the flour into a large mixing bowl then stir in the sugar.

Add the margarine and rub in until the mixture is crumbly, then stir in the sultanas.

Add enough milk to form a soft dough.

Divide the mixture into 12 rough heaps and place onto the prepared tray.

Bake in a moderately hot oven at 200°C (Conventional Electric Oven) for about 8-10 minutes until lightly golden brown.

Cool on a wire rack.

Iced Chocolate Cake

This is a surprisingly light chocolate cake recipe which has a thick layer of extremely chocolaty icing on top, enhancing the cake's taste. It is a quick and easy cake to make and is less involved than other chocolate cake recipes in this book such as the Rich Cherry Chocolate Cake Recipe.

Recipe Facts

Preparation Time: 40 minutes   Cooking Time: **20 minutes**

Dairy Free	Yes	**Gluten Free**	No
Egg Free	Yes	**Soya Free**	No
Nut Free	Yes	**Wheat Free**	No

Suitable for Freezing: **Yes**

Ingredients

185g non-dairy sunflower margarine
275g granulated sugar
35g cocoa powder, sifted
½ tsp baking powder
260ml soya milk
335g self-raising flour, sifted

For the chocolate icing:
125g icing sugar, sifted
60ml cold water (approx)
50g cocoa powder, sifted

Method

Grease a slab cake tin (20cm by 24cm) and line with baking parchment.

Into a medium sized saucepan, add the margarine, sugar, cocoa powder, baking powder and milk and stir over low heat until the margarine has melted and the sugar has dissolved. Bring to the boil then cool for about 10 minutes.

Add the sifted flour into the mixture and stir until smooth and there are no lumps of flour in the mixture. If desired, you can use a food processor to get it to a smooth consistency.

Spoon the mixture into the prepared tin.

Bake in a moderate oven at 180°C (Conventional Electric Oven) for about 20-23 minutes, depending on your oven, until the cake has just started to come away from the sides of the tin and when a skewer is gently placed into the centre of the cake it comes out clean.

Turn the cake out onto a wire rack and cool.

To make the chocolate icing add the icing sugar and a little water into a small bowl and stir until the icing sugar has dissolved. Add the cocoa powder and stir until smooth and there are no lumps.

Spread the cake with the chocolate icing once it has cooled.

Strawberry Surprise

These plain and simple looking little cakes have a lovely surprise inside when eaten…..an oozing puddle of sticky strawberry jam. The type of jam used in the center can easily be substituted for any other preferred as all will work well.

Recipe Facts

Preparation Time: 20 minutes   **Cooking Time: 8 minutes**

Dairy Free	Yes	**Gluten Free**	No
Egg Free	Yes	**Soya Free**	No
Nut Free	Yes	**Wheat Free**	No

Suitable for Freezing: **Yes**

Ingredients

250g self-raising flour, sifted
90g caster sugar
90g non-dairy sunflower margarine
45-60ml (3-4 tbsp) soya milk
Strawberry jam
Granulated sugar for sprinkling on top

Method

Line an oven tray with baking parchment.

Into a large mixing bowl add the flour then stir in the sugar.

Add the margarine and rub it in until the mixture is crumbly. Then add enough milk to form a soft dough.

Divide the dough into 12 portions and gently mould each one into a ball.

Make a small well in the centre of each ball and drop about a teaspoon of strawberry jam into each one.

Carefully mould the dough over the jam so the jam is now hidden. Brush with water and sprinkle with granulated sugar.

Bake in a moderately hot oven at 200°C (Conventional Electric Oven) for 8-10 minutes until lightly golden brown.

Cool on a wire rack.

Fruit Scones

With this recipe you can make either plain or fruit scones, both of which are scrumptious. They are delicious served with non-dairy sunflower margarine and a thick layer of jam. Best eaten on the day of making as they don't keep well.

Recipe Facts

Preparation Time: **20 minutes**   Cooking Time: **10 minutes**

Dairy Free	Yes	**Gluten Free**	No
Egg Free	Yes	**Soya Free**	No
Nut Free	Yes	**Wheat Free**	No

Suitable for Freezing: **Yes**

Ingredients

250g self-raising flour, sifted
60g granulated sugar
45g non-dairy sunflower margarine
60g raisins
75ml (5 tbsp) soya milk

Method

Line a large oven tray with baking parchment.

Add the flour and sugar into a mixing bowl then stir. Add the margarine and rub it in until the mixture is crumbly.

Add the raisins and mix well. Then add enough milk to form a soft dough.

Turn the dough out onto a lightly floured surface and knead gently for about 1-2 minutes. Roll the dough out until it's about an inch thick.

Cut into rounds using a cutter (2 inch in diameter). Place the rounds onto the prepared tray. Then re-roll excess dough and cut into rounds. Repeat until you have used all the dough.

Bake in a moderate oven at 220°C (Conventional Electric Oven) for about 10-12 minutes or until lightly golden brown, turning the tray around half way through the cooking time.

Best served warm with margarine and jam.

Date and Ginger Fairy Cakes

These are very tasty, very fruity fairy cakes. The combination of dates and ginger goes excellently together to add a fruity fragrance to these otherwise quite simple fairy cakes. They are quite moist and light little cakes, best eaten on the day of making them, or even better, warm from the oven.

Recipe Facts

Preparation Time: 30 minutes   Cooking Time: **15 minutes**

Dairy Free	Yes	**Gluten Free**	No
Egg Free	Yes	**Soya Free**	No
Nut Free	Yes	**Wheat Free**	No

Suitable for Freezing: **Yes**

Ingredients

90g non-dairy sunflower margarine
90g granulated sugar
90ml (6 tbsp) soya milk
185g self-raising flour, sifted
90g dates, chopped
30g glacé ginger, chopped

Method

Place 12 paper cake cases into a 12 hole bun tin.

Into a large mixing bowl cream together the margarine and sugar until light and fluffy. Then add 3 tbsp of milk and mix together.

Add the flour and mix well. You may want to use an electric hand whisk to make sure there are no lumps of flour in the mixture.

Add the dates and ginger and stir well. Add in 3 tbsp of milk and mix well.

Spoon the mixture into the prepared cake cases.

Bake in a moderate oven at 180°C (Conventional Electric Oven) for about 15-20 minutes, or until lightly golden brown.

Cool on a wire rack

Lemon Drizzle Cake

This lemon drizzle cake has a wonderful tangy flavour. The layers of light sponge cake are sandwiched together with lemon butter cream and the whole cake drizzled with tangy, lemon icing, making a delicious lemony feast. It also makes a great birthday cake. Best eaten on the day you make it.

Recipe Facts

Preparation Time: 40 minutes   **Cooking Time: 15 minutes**

Dairy Free	Yes	**Gluten Free**	No
Egg Free	Yes	**Soya Free**	No
Nut Free	Yes	**Wheat Free**	No

Suitable for Freezing: **Yes**

Ingredients

185g non-dairy sunflower margarine
185g granulated sugar
Grated rind of 2 lemons
1 tbsp lemon juice, freshly squeezed
105ml (7 tbsp) soya milk
375g self-raising flour, sifted

For the lemon cream:
Grated rind of 2 lemons
155g non-dairy sunflower margarine
90g icing sugar, sifted

For the lemon icing:
Grated rind of 1 lemon
Juice of half a lemon
Icing sugar, sifted

Method

Grease two deep 20cm round sandwich tins and line with baking parchment.

Cream together the margarine and sugar in a large mixing bowl until light and fluffy, then stir in the rind.

Add the lemon juice and milk. Stir well and do not worry if the mixture curdles.

Gradually add the flour, stirring well after each addition. You may want to use an electric hand whisk to make sure there are no lumps of flour left in the mixture.

Spoon the mixture equally into the prepared tins.

Bake in a moderate oven at 180°C (Conventional Electric Oven) for about 15-20 minutes, depending on your oven, until lightly golden brown and the cakes are just coming away from the sides of the tins. Check with a skewer, ensure it comes out clean when it is gently placed into the middle of the cakes.

Cool on a wire rack.

To make the lemon cream add the rind, margarine and sugar into a small bowl and mix until smooth and creamy.

To make the lemon icing add the rind and lemon juice into a small bowl and mix in enough icing sugar to make it the right consistency to spread.

Sandwich the cakes together with the lemon butter cream and then spread the top of the cake with the lemon icing.

Cranberry and Blueberry Sponge Cakes

Cranberries and blueberries are a great combination. Added into these little sponge cakes they make great little fruity sponge bites. If preferred, you can substitute the cranberries and blueberries for some raisins, sultanas or even some chopped apricots, most dried fruits will work well

Recipe Facts

Preparation Time: 30 minutes   **Cooking Time: 12 minutes**

Dairy Free	Yes		**Gluten Free**	No
Egg Free	Yes		**Soya Free**	No
Nut Free	Yes		**Wheat Free**	No

Suitable for Freezing: **Yes**

Ingredients

90g non-dairy sunflower margarine
90g granulated sugar
60-75ml (4-5 tbsp) soya milk
185g self-raising flour, sifted
30g dried cranberries
30g dried blueberries

Method

Place 12 paper cake cases into a 12 hole bun tin.

Cream together the margarine and sugar in a large mixing bowl until light and fluffy, then add the milk and mix well.

Add the sifted flour and stir well. You may want to use an electric hand blender or hand whisk to make sure there are no lumps of flour remaining.

Add the cranberries and blueberries and mix well.

Spoon the mixture into the prepared cake cases.

Bake in a moderate oven at 180°C (Conventional Electric Oven) for about 12-14 minutes or until lightly golden brown.

Cool on a wire rack.

Walnut Cake

This walnut cake is surprisingly moist and light, with a wonderful nutty flavour. As the nuts are ground before being added into the mixture, the wonderfully soft texture of the cake isn't interrupted, just enhanced in flavour. It's easy to make and so tasty it's definitely easy to eat!

Recipe Facts

Preparation Time: 30 minutes   **Cooking Time: 45 minutes**

Dairy Free	Yes		**Gluten Free**	No
Egg Free	Yes		**Soya Free**	No
Nut Free	No		**Wheat Free**	No

Suitable for Freezing: **Yes**

Ingredients

125g non-dairy sunflower margarine
220g granulated sugar
1 tsp vanilla extract
225g self-raising flour, sifted
170ml soya milk
70g walnuts, freshly ground

Method

Line a deep 18cm round cake tin with baking parchment.

Cream together the margarine and sugar in a large mixing bowl until light and fluffy, then stir in the vanilla extract.

Stir in the milk but do not worry if the mixture curdles.

Gradually add the flour, stirring well after each addition. You may want to use an electric hand whisk to make sure there are no lumps of flour in the mixture. Stir in the walnuts.

Spoon the mixture into the prepared tin.

Bake in a moderate oven at 180°C (Conventional Electric Oven) for about 40-50 minutes, depending on your oven, until the cake is browned and just coming away from the sides of the tin. Check with a skewer, ensure it comes out clean when it is gently placed into the middle of the cake.

Cool on a wire rack.

Eccles Cakes

These cakes are an old fashioned favourite and are delicious to eat either warm or cold. These flaky, tasty, sticky, sweet cakes make a lovely snack at all times of the day, including breakfast! They are relatively easy to cook and are one of my family's favourite cakes.

Recipe Facts

Preparation Time: 45 minutes   **Cooking Time: 12 minutes**

Dairy Free	Yes	**Gluten Free**	No
Egg Free	Yes	**Soya Free**	No
Nut Free	Yes	**Wheat Free**	No

Suitable for Freezing: Yes

Ingredients

60g dark muscovado sugar
125g raisins
45g mixed peel, chopped
60g non-dairy sunflower margarine
500g non-dairy ready made puff pastry
Granulated sugar for sprinkling

Method

Line a baking tray with baking parchment.

Add the muscavado sugar, raisins, mixed peel and margarine into a medium sized bowl. Mix well until evenly combined. This is the filling for the Eccles cakes.

Roll out the pastry on a lightly floured board until 26cm x 35mm (approximately) in size. Using a round pastry cutter (7 ½ cm in diameter) cut out a circle from the pastry.

Place a rounded teaspoon of filling into the centre of the pastry.

Carefully fold the pastry over until there is no gap for the filling to escape from. Press down gently until the raisins are nearly showing through the top of the pastry or it is about 5 ½ cm in diameter.

Place it on the prepared baking tray with the joins of the pastry facing the base of the tray.

Using a pair of scissors, make two slits in each of the cakes to let the air out.

Repeat the above 5 steps with the remaining pastry until there is no pastry left.

Cover the Eccles cakes with a tea towel and leave them to rest in a cool place for about 15 minutes.

Bake the cakes in a moderately hot oven at 200°C (Conventional Electric Oven) for about 12-15 minutes or until cooked through and lightly golden brown.

As soon as you have taken them out of the tray sprinkle them with sugar. Cool on the tray for about 15 minutes before transferring them onto a wire cooling rack to cool completely.

Chocolate Cup Cakes

These chocolate cup cakes are light to eat and very tasty, especially for the chocoholics amongst us. The mini chocolate sponges are covered in a thick layer of sticky chocolate icing making them a wonderful chocolaty snack. Quick and easy to make, they are great for children's birthday parties.

Recipe Facts

Preparation Time: **30 minutes**   Cooking Time: **15 minutes**

Dairy Free	Yes		**Gluten Free**	No
Egg Free	Yes		**Soya Free**	No
Nut Free	Yes		**Wheat Free**	No

Suitable for Freezing: **Yes**

Ingredients

125g non-dairy sunflower margarine
220g granulated sugar
45ml (3 tbsp) soya milk
45g desiccated coconut
300g self-raising flour, sifted
180ml orange juice
60g cocoa powder, sifted

For the chocolate icing:
125g icing sugar, sifted
60ml cold water (approx)
50g cocoa powder, sifted

Method

Place 24 paper cup cases into two 12-hole bun tins.

Cream together the margarine and sugar in a large mixing bowl, until light and fluffy.

Stir in the milk, but do not worry if the mixture curdles. You may want to use an electric hand whisk to mix in the milk.

Stir in the desiccated coconut, then stir in half the flour and half the orange juice and mix well. Mix in the cocoa powder.

Stir in the rest of the flour and orange juice until combined. You may want to use an electric hand whisk to make sure there are no lumps of flour in the mixture.

Spoon the mixture equally into the prepared paper cake cases.

Bake in a moderate oven at 180°C (Conventional Electric Oven) for about 15-20 minutes, depending on your oven, until cooked and when a skewer is placed into the middle of the cakes it comes out clean.

Cool the cakes on a wire rack.

To make the chocolate icing add the icing sugar and a little water into a small bowl and stir until the icing sugar has dissolved. Add the cocoa powder and stir until smooth and there are no lumps.

When the cakes are cold, spread the tops of the cakes with the chocolate icing.

Light Fruit Cake

This cake is packed full of fruit and sunflower seeds. Each mouthful seems to be a different combination of fruits and nuts, making it extremely tasty and sweet. It's quite a large cake so it's ideal for special occasions or even as a lighter version of a Christmas cake.

Recipe Facts

Preparation Time: 60 minutes   Cooking Time: **90 minutes**

Dairy Free	Yes	**Gluten Free**	No
Egg Free	Yes	**Soya Free**	No
Nut Free	No	**Wheat Free**	No

Suitable for Freezing: **Yes**

Ingredients

30g non-dairy sunflower margarine
165g granulated sugar
150g dried sour cherries, roughly chopped
150g dried apricots, chopped
75g glacé cherries, chopped
2 tsp ground cinnamon
½ nutmeg, grated
360ml cold water
85g walnuts, chopped
30g dried pineapple, chopped
25g dried papaya, chopped
25g dried mango, chopped
75g sunflower seeds
150g plain flour, sifted
150g self-raising flour, sifted
1 tsp baking powder
100ml water, extra

Method

Grease a deep 20cm round cake tin and line it with baking parchment.

Add the margarine, sugar, sour cherries, apricots, glacé cherries, cinnamon, nutmeg and the water into a large saucepan.

Place the saucepan over a low heat and stir until the sugar has dissolved. Then bring the mixture to the boil and simmer for 3 minutes, stirring occasionally. Take off the heat and cool to room temperature.

Add the walnuts, pineapple, papaya, mango and sunflower seeds into the mixture and stir well.

Add the plain flour and self-raising flour a little at a time, stirring well after each addition then add the baking powder and the extra 100ml of water. Stir the mixture really well using a large wooden spoon so that all the flour is well mixed in.

Spoon the mixture into the prepared tin.

Bake in a moderately slow oven at 160°C (Conventional Electric Oven) for about 1½ hours or until it's nicely browned and the cake is just coming away from the sides of the tin.

Turn the cake out onto a wire rack to cool.

Biscuits and Slices

Dark Rich Fruit Cookies

Christmas pudding in a cookie! These fruit cookies have a good helping of dried fruits as well as dark rum, nuts and treacle making them very tasty and quite similar in taste to Christmas pudding. They are great cookies all year round but especially at Christmas time.

Recipe Facts

Preparation Time: 30 minutes   **Cooking Time: 15 minutes**

Dairy Free	Yes	**Gluten Free**	No
Egg Free	Yes	**Soya Free**	No
Nut Free	No	**Wheat Free**	No

Suitable for Freezing: **Yes**

Ingredients

100g non-dairy sunflower margarine
150g dark muscovado sugar
2 tbsp treacle
1 tbsp dark rum
2-3 tbsp soya milk
150g plain flour, sifted
¼ tsp baking powder
45g rolled oats
50g pecans, chopped
50g walnuts, chopped
190g mixture of glacé cherries, dried apricots and dried sour cherries, chopped

Method

Line an oven tray with baking parchment.

Place into a large mixing bowl the margarine, sugar, treacle, rum and milk and mix until smooth. To help get the right consistency use either a food processor, blender or hand whisk.

Stir in the remaining ingredients.

Spoon level tablespoons of the mixture onto the prepared oven tray, about 5cm apart.

Bake in a moderate oven at 180°C (Conventional Electric Oven) for about 15-17 minutes or until browned.

Leave the cookies on the oven tray for about 5 minutes before placing them onto a wire rack to cool.

Rich Chocolate Cherry Cookies

These cookies are a great combination of chocolate and cherries, a match made in heaven. Each bite is a different combination of real dark chocolate chunks, soft cherries and crunchy nuts, all stuck together with a lovely soft cookie mix making them a real treat.

Recipe Facts

Preparation Time: 30 minutes   Cooking Time: **15 minutes**

Dairy Free	Yes	**Gluten Free**	No
Egg Free	Yes	**Soya Free**	No
Nut Free	No	**Wheat Free**	No

Suitable for Freezing: **Yes**

Ingredients

125g non-dairy sunflower margarine
1 tsp vanilla extract
250g dark muscovado sugar
45ml (3 tbsp) soya milk
150g plain flour, sifted
35g self-raising flour, sifted
1 tsp baking powder
35g cocoa powder, sifted
45g walnuts, chopped
45g pecan nuts, chopped
85g dried sour cherries, roughly chopped
100g dark chocolate, chopped

Method

Line an oven tray with baking parchment.

In a large mixing bowl cream together margarine, vanilla extract, sugar and milk until smooth.

Stir in the flours, baking powder and cocoa powder. Use a blender, food processor or a hand whisk to get the mixture to a smooth consistency.

Stir in the nuts, cherries and chocolate.

Drop slightly rounded tablespoons of the mixture onto the prepared oven tray, about 5cm apart.

Bake in a moderate oven at 180°C (Conventional Electric Oven) for about 15-17 minutes.

Cool on the tray.

Flap Jack

This is the simplest, easiest and quickest recipe in the book. Depending on how long it is cooked for, the flapjack can either be soft and chewy or crisp and crunchy, either way it is very tasty, especially covered in chocolate! Keeps really well for a few days in an airtight container.

Recipe Facts

Preparation Time: **15 minutes**   Cooking Time: **10 minutes**

Dairy Free	Yes	**Gluten Free**	No
Egg Free	Yes	**Soya Free**	Yes
Nut Free	Yes	**Wheat Free**	Yes

Suitable for Freezing: **Yes**

Ingredients

125g non-dairy sunflower margarine
125g demerara sugar
1 tbsp golden syrup
250g rolled oats

Method

Grease a Swiss roll tin and line with baking parchment.

Into a saucepan add the margarine, sugar and syrup. Stir over a low heat until the margarine has melted.

Take the sauce off the heat and add the oats. Stir the mixture well until all the oats are covered with the syrup/sugar mixture.

Press into the prepared tin.

Bake in a moderate oven at 180°C (Conventional Electric Oven) for about 10-12 minutes, depending on how crispy you like your flap jack.

Whilst the mixture is still warm and soft, lightly score the flap jack with a knife into squares. This will make it easier to cut the flap jack once it has cooled.

Variation

Follow the recipe above then melt 200g dark chocolate and spread over the flap jack whilst still warm. Once again, with a knife, score your chocolate flap jack into squares – chocolate flap jack!

Traditional Shortcake

This is one of my grandma's traditional recipes and she taught me how to make it. It's a very simple recipe, easy to make and quick to cook. As well as making plain traditional shortcake, there is also the option of adding some dried fruit to the mixture, for example raisins or cranberries, to make fruit shortcake. Both of these are great to eat especially when warm and crumbly!

Recipe Facts

Preparation Time: 20 minutes   **Cooking Time: 20 minutes**

Dairy Free	Yes	**Gluten Free**	No
Egg Free	Yes	**Soya Free**	Yes
Nut Free	Yes	**Wheat Free**	No

Suitable for Freezing: **Yes**

Ingredients

280g plain flour, sifted
90g granulated sugar
185g non-dairy sunflower margarine

Method

Line a large oven tray with baking parchment.

Into a large bowl add the flour and stir in the sugar.

Add the margarine and rub it in with your hands until the mixture resembles fine breadcrumbs.

Squeeze the mixture together to form a dough.

Cut the dough in half with a knife.

Place one half of the dough onto the prepared tray and using your hands, press into about a 7 inch round. Repeat this method with the other half of the dough.

Bake in a moderately hot oven at 200°C (Conventional Electric Oven) for about 17-20 minutes until lightly golden brown.

Whilst warm score into triangles. Cool on the tray.

Variations

Top the shortcake rounds with plain white icing (see section 'Sauces, Icings & Fillings').

OR

Add 60g of raisins or sultanas to the mixture and follow the recipe above.

OR

Sandwich the cold shortcake rounds together with strawberry jam and top with plain white icing (see section 'Sauces, Icings & Fillings').

Teatime Biscuits

As the name suggests these biscuits are great with afternoon tea. They are quite a plain biscuit with a subtle flavour of caraway seeds which makes them a little unusual from other biscuits. They are quick to cook which is great when you feel like a quick treat!

Recipe Facts

Preparation Time: 30 minutes   **Cooking Time: 7 minutes**

Dairy Free	Yes	**Gluten Free**	No
Egg Free	Yes	**Soya Free**	No
Nut Free	Yes	**Wheat Free**	No

Suitable for Freezing: **Yes**

Ingredients

250g non-dairy sunflower margarine
250g granulated sugar
375g self-raising flour, sifted
2 tsp caraway seeds
1 tsp cinnamon
15ml (1 tbsp) soya milk

Method

Line a large oven tray with baking parchment.

In a large mixing bowl, cream together the margarine and sugar until light and fluffy.

Add the flour, caraway seeds and cinnamon and mix well.

Add enough milk to form a soft dough.

Turn half of the dough out onto a floured work surface. Gently roll out the dough until 2-3mm thick. Cut into rounds using a cutter, approximately 6cm in diameter.

Using a lightly floured palette knife, carefully lift the rounds of dough onto the prepared tray. Re-roll the excess dough to make the remaining biscuits.

Repeat with the other half of the dough.

Bake in a moderately hot oven at 200°C (Conventional Electric Oven) for 6-7 minutes, (depending on your type of oven you may need to turn your tray around after approximately 3 minutes) until golden brown.

Cool on the tray. Dust with icing sugar if desired.

Oaty Walnut Biscuits

These oaty walnut biscuits are really easy to make and very tasty. The chopped walnuts add a lovely bite to these otherwise crumbly, melt in the mouth oat biscuits. You can substitute the walnuts with pecans if you prefer, both will work great in this recipe.

Recipe Facts

Preparation Time: 30 minutes   **Cooking Time: 10 minutes**

Dairy Free	Yes	**Gluten Free**	No
Egg Free	Yes	**Soya Free**	No
Nut Free	No	**Wheat Free**	No

Suitable for Freezing: **Yes**

Ingredients

185g non-dairy sunflower margarine
45g granulated sugar
15ml (1tbsp) soya milk
185g plain flour, sifted
1tsp baking powder
45g rolled oats
45g chopped walnuts

Method

Line a baking tray with baking parchment

In a large mixing bowl cream together the margarine and sugar until light and fluffy.

Add the soya milk and stir well.

Add the flour and baking powder and stir well. Use an electric hand whisk to make sure there are no lumps of flour in the mixture.

Add the rolled oats and stir well.

Add the walnuts and stir well.

Place dessert spoon size balls of the mixture onto the prepared baking tray.

Bake in a moderate oven at 180°C (Conventional Electric Oven) for about 10 minutes (turning the tray around half way through cooking) or until lightly golden brown.

Cool on the tray.

Passion Fruit Cookies

These passion fruit cookies consist of two slightly chewy, tangy biscuits sandwiched together with a soft passion fruit butter cream. Both biscuit and cream have a soft crunch provided by the passion fruit seeds offering a lovely combination of textures and flavours. They are quite involved to make so you will need to set aside some time to make them, but they are well worth it.

Recipe Facts

Preparation Time: 50 minutes   **Cooking Time: 6 minutes**

Dairy Free	Yes	**Gluten Free**	No
Egg Free	Yes	**Soya Free**	No
Nut Free	Yes	**Wheat Free**	No

Suitable for Freezing: **Yes**

Ingredients

125g non-dairy sunflower margarine
110g granulated sugar
2 tbsp golden syrup
150g self-raising flour, sifted
100g plain flour, sifted
½ tsp ground ginger
30g glacé ginger
Pulp of 2 small passion fruit
15ml (1 tbsp) soya milk (optional)

For the passion fruit cream:
60g non-dairy sunflower margarine
120g icing sugar, sifted
Pulp of 1 small passion fruit

Method

Line a baking tray with baking parchment.

In a large mixing bowl cream together the margarine and sugar until light and fluffy. Add the syrup and mix well.

Add the flours and ground ginger and stir well. Use and electric hand whisk to make sure there are no lumps of flour in the mixture.

Add the glacé ginger and passion fruit pulp and stir well. The mixture may now have formed a soft dough, if not add the milk and mix well until it does form a soft dough.

Turn the dough out onto a lightly floured surface and knead lightly for about a minute. Roll the dough out in between two sheets of unbleached baking powder, until about 2-3mm thick.

Using a biscuit cutter (2 inch in diameter), cut the dough into rounds. Using a floured palette knife, gently place the biscuits onto the prepared tray.

Repeat the previous 2 steps until there is no dough left.

Bake in a moderate oven at 180°C (Conventional Electric Oven) for about 6-7 minutes, turning them round after about 4 minutes, until lightly golden brown.

Cool on the tray.

To make the passion fruit cream add the margarine and icing sugar into a small bowl and mix until smooth and creamy. Add the passion fruit pulp and stir well.

Lightly spread half the cold biscuits with the passion fruit cream. Place the remaining biscuits on top to sandwich them together. Dust with icing sugar if desired.

Orange & Apricot Squares

The combination of orange and apricot makes for a great tasting slice. The tangy, gooey topping compliments the soft and moist cake underneath. Citrus tang and sticky apricots really stand out in this slice, and are an excellent combination of flavours. Will keep quite well for a few days in an airtight container.

Recipe Facts

Preparation Time: **40 minutes**   Cooking Time: **15 minutes**

Dairy Free	Yes	**Gluten Free**	No
Egg Free	Yes	**Soya Free**	No
Nut Free	Yes	**Wheat Free**	No

Suitable for Freezing: **Yes**

Ingredients

125g non-dairy sunflower margarine
200g light muscovado sugar
Grated rind of 1 large orange
60ml (4 tbsp) soya milk
220g self-raising flour, sifted
2 tbsp orange juice
235g dried apricots, chopped

For the orange icing:
185g icing sugar, sifted
30ml orange juice
Grated rind of 1 large orange

Method

Grease a Swiss roll tin and line with baking parchment.

In a large mixing bowl, cream together the margarine and sugar until light and fluffy. Add the rind and milk and stir well.

Add the flour and stir well. Use an electric hand whisk to make sure there are no lumps of flour in the mixture.

Add the orange juice and stir, then add the apricots and stir well.

Spoon the mixture into the prepared tin.

Bake in a moderate oven at 180°C (Conventional Electric Oven) for 15-20 minutes depending on your oven, or until it has just started to come away from the sides of the tin and is lightly golden brown.

Leave to stand in the tin for about 5 minutes before turning it out onto a wire rack to cool.

To make the orange icing add the rind and icing sugar into a small bowl and stir well. Gradually add the orange juice stirring well after each addition.

Spread the cooled cake with the orange icing.

Cherry and Coconut loaf

This moist and tasty loaf is quite an easy one to make. The coconut offers great flavour but makes the spongy cake mixture slightly more dense than other cakes, while the glacé cherries make a lovely sweet addition to each bite. As it is quite moist it will keep well for a couple of days in an airtight container.

Recipe Facts

Preparation Time: **25 minutes**   Cooking Time: **35 minutes**

Dairy Free	Yes		**Gluten Free**	No
Egg Free	Yes		**Soya Free**	No
Nut Free	Yes		**Wheat Free**	No

Suitable for Freezing: **Yes**

Ingredients

280g self-raising flour, sifted
125g non-dairy sunflower margarine
75g desiccated coconut
125g granulated sugar
140g glacé cherries, roughly chopped
220ml soya milk

Method

Grease a loaf dish (13cm wide x 7cm high x 23cm long) and line it with baking parchment.

Into a large mixing bowl add the flour and rub in the margarine with your hands until the mixture resembles fine breadcrumbs.

Stir in the coconut, sugar and cherries and mix well.

Stir in the soya milk and mix well until combined.

Spoon the mixture into the prepared dish.

Bake in a moderate oven at 180°C (Conventional Electric Oven) for about 35-40 minutes or until golden brown and cooked through.

Cool in the dish to room temperature before turning it out onto a wire cooling rack.

Jam tarts

These jam tarts are very easy to make. They can be eaten warm for a dessert with custard or just as a snack at anytime time of the day. They are made here with strawberry jam but this can easily be substituted for any jam of your choice for example, Victoria plum or raspberry. They are great for parties as you can make them in advance and freeze them.

Recipe Facts

Preparation Time: 20 minutes   Cooking Time: **12 minutes**

Dairy Free	Yes	**Gluten Free**	No
Egg Free	Yes	**Soya Free**	Yes
Nut Free	Yes	**Wheat Free**	No

Suitable for Freezing: **Yes**

Ingredients

500g ready made non-dairy short crust pastry
Strawberry jam or any jam of your choice

Method

Grease two 12 hole bun tins.

Roll out the pastry on a lightly floured board until 26cm x 35cm (approximately).

Cut the pastry into circles using a pastry cutter (7 ½ cm in diameter).

Place the circles of pastry into the prepared tin.

Place about 1 tsp of jam into the centre of each of the pastry cases.

Repeat the above steps until there is no pastry left.

Bake in a moderately hot oven at 200°C (Conventional Electric Oven) for about 12-15 minutes or until lightly golden brown.

Leave the tarts in the tray for about 10 minutes before turning them out onto a wire rack to cool.

Fruity Flapjacks

These flap jacks are very easy to make and certainly moreish. Deliciously fruity and soft, these flapjacks are mouthwatering bites. If you do not like honey you can substitute it for golden syrup and it will work just as well. They will keep well for a few days in an air tight container.

Recipe Facts

Preparation Time: 25 minutes   Cooking Time: **15 minutes**

Dairy Free	Yes	**Gluten Free**	No
Egg Free	Yes	**Soya Free**	Yes
Nut Free	Yes	**Wheat Free**	Yes

Suitable for Freezing: **Yes**

Ingredients

155g rolled oats
90g raisins
90g dried apricots, chopped
125g granulated sugar
75g self-raising flour, sifted
155g non-dairy sunflower margarine, melted
1 tbsp runny honey

Method

Grease a Swiss roll tin or a lamington tin and line it with baking parchment.

Into a mixing bowl add the oats, raisins, apricots, sugar and flour and stir well.

Add the melted margarine and honey and mix well until combined.

Spoon the mixture into the prepared tin and level it out so the mixture is evenly distributed over the tin.

Bake in a moderate oven at 180°C (Conventional Electric Oven) for about 15 minutes or until lightly golden brown.

Whilst the mixture is still warm and soft, lightly score the flap jack with a knife into squares. This will make it easier to cut the flap jack once it has cooled.

Lemon Cream Biscuits

These lemon cream biscuits are a lovely sandwich of melt in the mouth biscuit and soft lemon cream. They are tangy, light to eat and delicious with a lovely fresh tasting lemony flavour provided by the zest in the icing and cream.

Recipe Facts

Preparation Time: 30 minutes   Cooking Time: **6 minutes**

Dairy Free	Yes	**Gluten Free**	No
Egg Free	Yes	**Soya Free**	No
Nut Free	Yes	**Wheat Free**	No

Suitable for Freezing: **Yes**

Ingredients

125g granulated sugar
250g self-raising flour, sifted
Grated rind of 1 lemon
125g non-dairy sunflower margarine
30ml (2 tbsp) soya milk

For the lemon cream:
Grated rind of 2 lemons
155g non-dairy sunflower margarine
90g icing sugar, sifted

For the lemon icing:
Grated rind of 1 lemon
Juice of half a lemon
Icing sugar, sifted

Method

Line an oven tray with baking parchment.

In a large mixing bowl stir together the sugar, flour and lemon rind. Add the margarine and mix with your hands until the mixture resembles fine breadcrumbs.

Add the milk and mix to form a dough.

Lightly knead half the dough on a floured work surface, and then roll it out until it is a few millimetres thick. Cut into rounds using a medium sized pastry cutter then using a floured palette knife carefully place them onto the prepared oven tray.

Bake in a moderately hot oven at 200°C (Conventional Electric Oven) for about 6-8 minutes (depending on how crunchy you like your biscuits) until lightly browned.

Cool on trays. While the biscuits are cooling make the lemon icing and lemon cream

To make the lemon cream add the rind, margarine and sugar into a small bowl and mix until smooth and creamy.

To make the lemon icing take a small bowl and add the rind and lemon juice. Then mix in enough icing sugar to make it the right consistency.

Sandwich the cold biscuits with the lemon cream and top with the lemon icing.

Variations

Sandwich the biscuits together with a layer of plain butter cream (see section 'Sauces, Icings & Fillings') and strawberry jam and top with plain white icing (see section 'Sauces, Icings & Fillings').

Vanillas

These pastries are so light you could eat several in one go! The vanilla custard provides an excellent filling for the two pastry slices, and the soft icing on top finishes them off perfectly. They can be prepared during the day and made up just before serving so it is ideal for making at dinner parties. They do not keep well so they are best eaten on the day you make them.

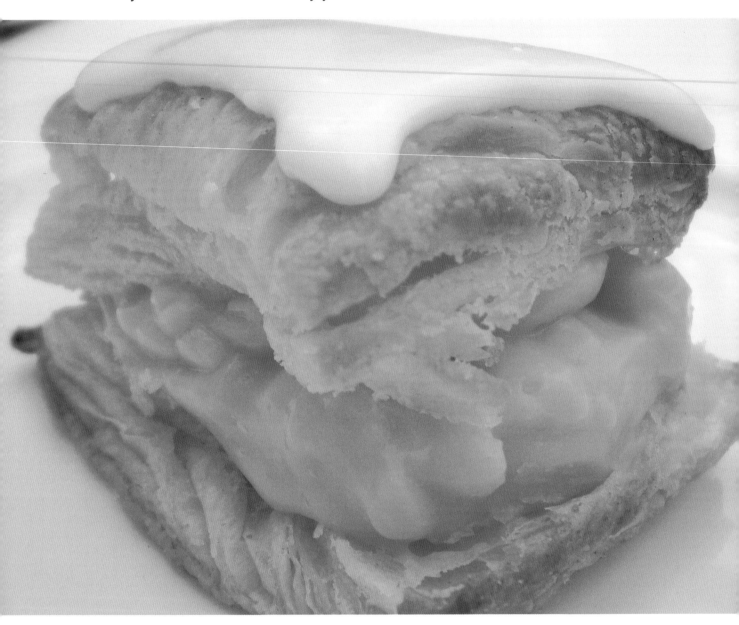

Recipe Facts

Preparation Time: **50 minutes**   Cooking Time: **20 minutes**

Dairy Free	Yes	**Gluten Free**	No
Egg Free	Yes	**Soya Free**	No
Nut Free	Yes	**Wheat Free**	No

Suitable for Freezing: **No**

Ingredients

500g non-dairy ready made puff pastry

For the vanilla custard:
3 tbsp granulated sugar
3 tbsp custard powder
900ml soya milk
1 ½ tsp vanilla extract

For the plain white icing:
200g icing sugar, sifted
30ml water (approx)

Method

Roll out the pastry until it is about a 26cm by 40cm rectangle, lightly dusting the board and the pastry with flour so it does not stick to the board or the rolling pin.

Cut the pastry into as big or as small rectangles/squares as you desire. I would recommend cutting the pastry into about 8½cm by 9½cm rectangles for a reasonable sized vanilla. This will make roughly 12 rectangles (6 vanillas).

Bake in a moderately hot oven at 200°C (Conventional Electric Oven) for about 15-20 minutes or until cooked and lightly golden brown.

Cool on a wire rack. Whilst the pastry is cooling you can make the vanilla custard.

To make the vanilla custard take a 2 pint measuring jug and mix together the sugar, custard powder and a little milk until smooth. Add the rest of the milk and stir.

Pour into a small medium based saucepan. Stir the mixture constantly over a medium heat until thickened.

Once it has thickened remove it from the heat and stir in the vanilla extract.

Cool to room temperature and then place in the fridge for a couple of hours or until it has set and is cold.

To make the plain white icing add icing sugar and a little water into a small bowl and stir until icing sugar has dissolved and it's the right consistency to spread.

When the pastry is cold, carefully spread the plain white icing on top of one of the rectangles of pastry and leave it until the icing has set.

Once the icing has set, spoon cold vanilla custard onto another rectangle of pastry then gently place the iced pastry rectangle on top of the custard.

Repeat the above 2 steps until you have run out of pastry and all are assembled.

Iced Coconut Cherry Slice

This slice is quite sweet to eat and goes really well with non-dairy ice cream. It is packed full of coconut and glacé cherries making it a sweet, sticky, crumbly and very tasty slice.

Recipe Facts

Preparation Time: 45 minutes   Cooking Time: **20 minutes**

Dairy Free	Yes	**Gluten Free**	No
Egg Free	Yes	**Soya Free**	No
Nut Free	Yes	**Wheat Free**	No

Suitable for Freezing: **Yes**

Ingredients

For the pastry:
90g non-dairy sunflower margarine
60g granulated sugar
15-30ml (1-2 tbsp) soya milk
½ tsp vanilla extract
155g self-raising flour, sifted
30g cornflour

For the icing:
185g icing sugar, sifted
30ml (2 tbsp) soya milk (approx)

For the filling:
190g desiccated coconut
220g granulated sugar
125g glacé cherries, roughly chopped
135ml (9 tbsp) soya milk

Method

Grease a lamington tin (28cm x 18cm) and line it with baking parchment.

To make the pastry cream together the margarine and sugar in a large mixing bowl until light and fluffy.

Add the milk and vanilla extract and stir well.

Add the self-raising flour and cornflour. Mix well until a soft dough has formed. Cut the dough in half.

Roll one half of the dough in between two sheets of baking parchment until it is approximately 28cm x 18cm in size and fits the base of the prepared lamington tin.

Remove the baking parchment and place the pastry onto the base of the prepared tin.

Roll the other half of the dough between two sheets of baking parchment until it is 28cm x 18cm, and place it aside as it will go on top of the filling.

To make the filling add the coconut, sugar, cherries and milk into a large mixing bowl.

Mix well until combined and the cherries are evenly distributed.

Spoon the filling over the pastry in the tin and spread the mixture evenly.

Carefully place the pastry which has been set aside over the filling, making sure it has all been covered, and remove the baking parchment in the process.

Bake in a moderate oven at 180°C (Conventional Electric Oven) for about 20 minutes or until it is lightly golden brown.

Cool in the tin.

Whilst it is cooling you can make the icing.

To make the icing add the icing sugar and milk into a small bowl and stir well until combined.

Once the slice has cooled down to room temperature spread the icing evenly over the top and leave it to set.

After the icing has set cut the slice into squares.

Christmas

Christmas Cake

This is a very tasty fruit cake which is quite light to eat and keeps really well for days if stored in an airtight container. It's quite a large cake so there is plenty to go round at Christmas. I would recommend making it in a day or so in advance so there is enough time for you to decorate it. However, you could also make it a few weeks beforehand, wrap it up and put it in the freezer. This also makes a great Christening or Wedding Cake.

Recipe Facts

Preparation Time: 90 minutes   Cooking Time: **2½ hours**

Dairy Free	Yes	**Gluten Free**	No
Egg Free	Yes	**Soya Free**	No
Nut Free	No	**Wheat Free**	No

Suitable for Freezing: **Yes**

Ingredients

385g dried apricots, chopped
330g raisins
140g glacé cherries, chopped
100g dried pineapple, chopped
15g dried sour cherries
185g non-dairy sunflower margarine
200g dark muscovado sugar
250ml cold water
125ml dark rum
60ml Victoria plum jam
135ml (9 tbsp) soya milk
365g self-raising flour, sifted
85g plain flour, sifted

For the decoration:
2 tsp strawberry jam (approx)
908g ready to roll golden marzipan
908g ready to roll white icing

Method

Line a deep 19cm square cake tin with two layers of baking parchment.

To make the cake add the apricots, raisins, glacé cherries, pineapple, dried cherries, margarine, sugar and water into a large saucepan. Stir well over a low heat until the sugar has dissolved and the margarine has melted.

Bring the mixture to the boil, stirring occasionally so the mixture does not stick to the base of the pan. Turn the heat down, cover the pan and simmer for about 10 minutes, stirring occasionally.

Add the rum and jam and mix well. Leave the mixture to cool to room temperature.

Add the milk and stir well.

Gradually stir in the self-raising flour and plain flour. Mix very well until all the flour has been mixed in.

Spoon the mixture into the prepared tin and bake in a moderately slow oven at 160°C (Conventional Electric Oven) for about 2½ hours depending on your oven.

Cover with foil and cool in the tin.

To prepare the jam layer warm approximately 2 tsp of strawberry jam.

Spread the jam thinly over the cake, on the top and around the sides. If the top of your cake is not quite level then trim it slightly so it is.

To prepare the marzipan roll out the golden marzipan, using icing sugar to stop it sticking to the board, to about 13 inch square.

Carefully place the marzipan onto the cake which has already been spread thinly with jam.

Trim the edges of the marzipan.

To prepare the icing roll out the ready to roll white icing, using icing sugar to stop it sticking to the board, to about 13 inch square.

Carefully place the icing over the marzipan.

Trim the edges of the icing.

Mince Pies

These mince pies are delicious served warm with either custard or non-dairy vanilla ice cream, but also work very well cold. Instead of filling the pies with mincemeat you can use a type of jam, for example strawberry, and turn them into mini jam pies! They are classically served at Christmas time but I like to eat them all year round.

Recipe Facts

Preparation Time: 25 minutes   **Cooking Time: 17 minutes**

Dairy Free	Yes	**Gluten Free**	No
Egg Free	Yes	**Soya Free**	Yes
Nut Free	Yes	**Wheat Free**	No

Suitable for Freezing: **Yes**

Ingredients

500g ready made non-dairy short crust pastry
Small jar of classic mincemeat

Method

Grease a 12 hole bun tray.

Roll out the pastry on a lightly floured board until approximately 26cm x 35cm.

Cut the pastry into 12 circles using a pastry cutter (7 ½ cm in diameter). These will be the base and sides of the pies.

Place the circles of pastry into the prepared tin.

On a lightly floured board, roll out the left over pastry you have from making the bases until it's approximately 2mm thick.

Cut the pastry into circles using a pastry cutter (6cm in diameter). These will be the tops of the pies. You may have to re-roll the pastry again until you have 12 circles.

Place about 1 tsp of mincemeat into the middle of each of the 12 pastry cases.

Place the circles of pastry which were reserved for the tops over the mincemeat.

Gently press down the tops of the pies and create a small hole in it using a skewer.

Bake in a moderately hot oven at 200°C (Conventional Electric Oven) for about 17-20 minutes or until lightly golden brown.

Leave the pies in the tray for about 10 minutes before turning them out onto a wire rack to cool.

Repeat the above steps until you have no more pastry left, making sure the baking tin has cooled down to room temperature before placing uncooked pastry in it.

Mincemeat Squares

This is an ideal slice to make at Christmas time instead of mince pies. It's soft and sticky texture makes it great to eat on its own, either warm or cold, but it also makes a great dessert served warm with custard. Instead of putting mincemeat in the middle you could use strawberry jam or any jam of your choice, which works well and is just as delicious.

Recipe Facts

Preparation Time: 30 minutes   Cooking Time: **20 minutes**

Dairy Free	Yes	**Gluten Free**	No
Egg Free	Yes	**Soya Free**	No
Nut Free	Yes	**Wheat Free**	No

Suitable for Freezing: **Yes**

Ingredients

500g self-raising flour, sifted
250g granulated sugar
250g non-dairy sunflower margarine
60ml (4 tbsp) soya milk
410g classic mincemeat
Demerara sugar for sprinkling on top

Method

Grease a Swiss roll tin or a lamington tin and line it with baking parchment.

Into a large mixing bowl add the flour and sugar and mix well. Add the margarine and rub it in until the mixture is crumbly, then add enough milk to form a soft dough.

Place the dough on a floured work surface and knead lightly for a minute or two.

Cut the dough in half with a knife and press one half into the base of the prepared tin.

Roll the other half of the dough in between 2 sheets of baking parchment until you have the right size to cover the top of the tin.

Carefully spread the mincemeat over the dough that's in the base of the tin.

Gently lift the other half of the dough up and it place over the mincemeat removing all of the baking parchment. Do not worry if some of the dough breaks off, just piece it back together again in the tin.

Brush the top with milk and sprinkle with demerara sugar.

Bake in a moderate oven at 180°C (Conventional Electric Oven) for 20-25 minutes until it is lightly golden brown. Serve.

Variation

Instead of using mincemeat you could use any jam of your choice.

Christmas Pudding

This is a very traditional recipe, which makes a surprisingly light pudding. It is delicious served warm with rum sauce. It's best made about 6 weeks in advance of Christmas but it can be made up to 3 weeks before. It's a great way to end your Christmas dinner.

Recipe Facts

Preparation Time: 60 minutes   Cooking Time: **4 hours**

Dairy Free	Yes	**Gluten Free**	No
Egg Free	Yes	**Soya Free**	No
Nut Free	Yes	**Wheat Free**	No

Suitable for Freezing: **No**

Ingredients

250g self-raising flour, sifted
125g light vegetable suet
125g dried sour cherries
125g soft dried figs, chopped
125g dried apricots, chopped
125g fresh white breadcrumbs
125g demerara sugar
2 tbsp black treacle
½ tsp baking powder
½ tsp mixed spice
45ml (3 tbsp) dark rum
180ml (12 tbsp) soya milk

Method

Grease a 2 pint pudding basin.

Add the flour, suet, fruit, breadcrumbs, sugar, treacle, baking powder and mixed spice into a large mixing bowl and stir very well. Then add the rum and milk and mix well using a large wooden spoon until combined. Spoon the mixture into the prepared pudding basin.

Cover with baking parchment and tie string around the rim of the basin so as to keep the baking parchment in place. Tie the string very tightly so the baking parchment does not come off whilst cooking.

Cover the baking parchment with a piece of tinfoil. Tie a piece of string around the rim of the basin to keep the tinfoil in place. Tie the string tightly so the tinfoil does not come off whilst cooking.

Make a handle with a piece of string and attach it to the bowl. This is to make it easier to lift the pudding out of the pan which you are going to steam it in.

Place the pudding into a large pan which is suitable for steaming the pudding in. Pour in about 1 ½ to 2 inches of water. Make sure you do not put too much water in as it may bubble up into the pudding.

Steam the pudding for about 4 hours. Check the water level about every 20 minutes to make sure the water has not boiled away, otherwise, if there is no water left to steam, the base of your pan will burn as well as the base of your pudding. Therefore, you must make sure you keep adding a little water so there is always enough, but not too much, to steam.

Once the pudding is cooked leave it in the basin for about 3 to 6 weeks or until Christmas day.

Desserts and Puddings

Mango Pudding

This is a delicious hot winter pudding and great served with custard. The sticky, toffee like topping is a fantastic contrast to the soft gooey mango underneath. The leftovers (if there are any) are just as good to eat cold. You can also make it with peaches, nectarines or cooking apples instead of mangoes.

Recipe Facts

Preparation Time: 40 minutes   **Cooking Time: 40 minutes**

Dairy Free	Yes	**Gluten Free**	No
Egg Free	Yes	**Soya Free**	No
Nut Free	Yes	**Wheat Free**	No

Suitable for Freezing: **No**

Ingredients

For the filling:
4 large mangoes (smooth variety), peeled, stone removed and cut into large pieces
8 tsp demerara sugar
2 tsp vanilla extract
120ml (8 tbsp) cold water

For the topping:
280g non-dairy sunflower margarine
280g granulated sugar
280g self-raising flour, sifted
75-90ml (5-6 tbsp) soya milk

Method

Preheat the oven to 180°C (Conventional Electric Oven).

To make the filling place the mango into a deep oven proof dish (23cm by 30cm). Sprinkle the demerara sugar over the mango and then add the vanilla extract and water. Gently stir together.

Place it into the preheated oven for 10 minutes whilst you make the topping.

To make the topping cream together the margarine and sugar in a large mixing bowl until light and fluffy.

Add the flour and mix well until it is a smooth consistency with no lumps of flour remaining. You can use an electric blender, a food processor or a hand whisk to make sure there are no lumps in the mixture.

Add enough milk to make it a dropping consistency i.e. so the mixture slowly drops off the spoon.

Take the dish with the mangoes in out of the oven and spread the topping mixture over the mangoes.

Bake in a moderate oven at 180°C (Conventional Electric Oven) for 40-45 minutes until it is golden brown.

Serve warm, with custard if you prefer.

Variation

Use 3 large cooking apples instead of the mangoes. Peel, core and slice the apples then follow the recipe above.

Chocolate Mousse

This chocolate mousse is a quick dessert to make but you have to wait a few hours for the mousse to set so it will need preparing in advance. It's ideal for a party as chocolate mousse is a sure favourite, especially with children.

Recipe Facts

Preparation Time: 30 minutes   Cooking Time: **10 minutes**

Dairy Free	Yes		**Gluten Free**	No
Egg Free	Yes		**Soya Free**	No
Nut Free	Yes		**Wheat Free**	Yes

Suitable for Freezing: **No**

Ingredients

4 level tbsp cornflour
4 level tbsp cocoa powder, sifted
105ml (7 tbsp) soya milk
900ml soya milk extra
10 rounded tbsp granulated sugar
60g non-dairy sunflower margarine

Method

Into a 1 pint measuring jug add the cornflour and cocoa powder and mix well. Add the 7 tbsp of milk and mix to a smooth paste, making sure there are no lumps.

Pour 1½ pints of milk into a medium sized saucepan. Slowly bring it to the boil, stirring occasionally.

Add the paste to the hot milk and beat with a hand whisk until there are no lumps.

Bring the mixture to the boil, whisking it all the time. Boil it for about 2 minutes.

Turn the heat down to its lowest setting then add the sugar and the margarine. Whisk the mixture well for about 3 minutes.

Use an electric hand blender or a hand whisk to remove any remaining lumps and to make sure the mixture is light and airy.

Pour immediately into an ovenproof glass dish.

Cool to room temperature.

Cover the dish and place it in the fridge. Allow it to set before serving.

Vanilla Custard Cake

This is quite an unusual dessert as you cook the teacake with custard actually inside it. It is delicious to eat as the vanilla and custard complement each other excellently, whilst the crumbly sponge provides the perfect wrapper for the soft center. It is quite a rich cake so you only need a small piece. It will keep well for a day or two.

Recipe Facts

Preparation Time: **40 minutes**   Cooking Time: **30 minutes**

Dairy Free	Yes	**Gluten Free**	No
Egg Free	Yes	**Soya Free**	No
Nut Free	Yes	**Wheat Free**	No

Suitable for Freezing: **No**

Ingredients

For the cake mixture:
125g non-dairy sunflower margarine
70g granulated sugar
45ml (3 tbsp) soya milk
110g self-raising flour, sifted
45g custard powder

For the custard:
1 tbsp custard powder
1 tbsp granulated sugar
170ml soya milk
15g non-dairy sunflower margarine
2tsp vanilla extract

Method

Grease a round ovenproof glass pie dish (20cm in diameter and 3cm deep).

To make the cake mixture cream together the margarine and sugar in a mixing bowl until light and fluffy. Add the milk and mix well.

Stir in the flour and custard powder and mix until smooth. Use an electric blender, food processor or hand whisk to remove any remaining lumps of flour.

Spread half the mixture over the base and up the sides of the prepared dish.

To make the custard add the custard powder and sugar into a small saucepan then stir. Add a little of the milk and mix well until there are no lumps. Add the remaining milk and stir well.

Bring the mixture to the boil and stir constantly until the mixture has thickened. Remove from the heat and stir in margarine and vanilla extract.

Cool to room temperature.

To make the cake spoon the custard into the prepared dish with the cake mixture in and spread evenly. Carefully spread the rest of the cake mixture on top of the custard.

Bake in a moderate oven at 180°C (Conventional Electric Oven) for about 30-35 minutes until lightly golden.

Serve warm.

Pineapple Syrup Sponge Pudding

An upside down cake looks very impressive if turned out correctly but is well worth the risk. This pineapple pudding is a great combination of juicy fruit and syrupy, sticky sponge. Goes very well with either custard or non-dairy cream for a great family dessert.

Recipe Facts

Preparation Time: **45 minutes**   Cooking Time: **40 minutes**

Dairy Free	Yes	**Gluten Free**	No
Egg Free	Yes	**Soya Free**	No
Nut Free	Yes	**Wheat Free**	No

Suitable for Freezing: **No**

Ingredients

7 rings of tinned pineapple
13 glacé cherries
3-4 tbsp golden syrup
125g non-dairy sunflower margarine
125g granulated sugar
185g self-raising flour, sifted
75ml (5 tbsp) soya milk

Method

In a round fluted flan dish (23cm in diameter and about 3cm deep) arrange the pineapple rings over the base. Add a cherry into the middle of each of the pineapple rings and also into the gaps in between each ring around the edge.

Drizzle the syrup over the pineapple and cherries.

Put the margarine and sugar into a mixing bowl and cream them together until light and fluffy.

Add the flour and mix well until it has combined and there are no lumps of flour in the mixture. Use an electric hand whisk or food processor to remove any remaining lumps of flour.

Add the milk and mix until it's a smooth dropping consistency i.e. the mixture slowly drops off the spoon.

Spoon the mixture over the pineapple and the cherries.

Bake in a moderate oven at 180°C (Conventional Electric Oven) for about 40-45 minutes until golden brown.

Serve warm with custard if preferred.

Apple and Cinnamon Pudding

This is a delicious hot apple pudding, which can be served either with ice cream or custard. The topping has a rich treacley taste which contrasts well with the sharper apple flavour. The tastier the apples you use, the better the pudding and I find home grown Bramley apples are the best. It keeps quite well for a couple of days, but it's obviously best served warm straight from the oven!

Recipe Facts

Preparation Time: **45 minutes**   Cooking Time: **45 minutes**

Dairy Free	Yes	**Gluten Free**	No
Egg Free	Yes	**Soya Free**	Yes
Nut Free	No	**Wheat Free**	No

Suitable for Freezing: **No**

Ingredients

For the base:
125g self-raising flour, sifted
30g ground almonds
90g non-dairy sunflower margarine
60g dark muscovado sugar
2 tsp lemon juice

For the topping:
60g plain flour, sifted
155g dark muscovado sugar
60g non-dairy sunflower margarine
1½ tsp ground cinnamon

For the filling:
500g cooking apples, peeled, cored and sliced
90g dark muscovado sugar
Grated rind and juice of 1 lemon

Method

Grease a glass pie dish (20cm in diameter and 2½ cm deep).

To make the base add the flour and almonds into a mixing bowl then stir. Add the margarine and rub in until the mixture is crumbly.

Stir in the sugar and lemon juice and mix well.

Spread the mixture onto the base of the dish and up the sides.

To make the filling mix together the apples, sugar, rind and lemon juice in a bowl and stir well.

To make the topping add the flour and sugar into a mixing bowl and stir. Add the margarine and cinnamon and mix well until the mixture is crumbly.

To make the pudding spoon the apples into the prepared dish with the mixture already in, then sprinkle the topping over the apples.

Bake in a moderate oven at 180°C (Conventional Electric Oven) for about 45-50 minutes.

Serve warm.

Strawberry Custard Flan

This is a fabulous summer dessert, especially when the English strawberries are in season. It is quite a light dessert, encompassing a whole combination of textures from crisp pastry and soft custard to fresh juicy fruit. It's relatively easy to make but takes quite a long time to set as it needs to cool in the fridge. As it contains strawberries and custard, it is best eaten on the day of making it.

Recipe Facts

Preparation Time: 60 minutes   **Cooking Time: 15 minutes**

Dairy Free	Yes	**Gluten Free**	No
Egg Free	Yes	**Soya Free**	No
Nut Free	Yes	**Wheat Free**	No

Suitable for Freezing: **No**

Ingredients

For the pastry and filling:
185g plain flour, sifted
60g granulated sugar
125g non-dairy sunflower margarine
15ml (1 tbsp) soya milk
500g strawberries, hulled and sliced

For the custard:
2 level tbsp granulated sugar
2 rounded tbsp custard powder
600ml soya milk

Method

Grease a round fluted flan dish (23cm in diameter and about 3cm deep).

To make the pastry add the flour and sugar into a large mixing bowl and stir. Add the margarine and rub it in until the mixture is crumbly. Add the milk and mix well to form a soft dough.

Turn the dough out onto a lightly floured work surface and gently knead it for about 2 minutes.

Place the dough on a plate and cover it with cling film, then put it in a fridge for about 30 minutes. Press the dough into the flan dish so it covers the base and sides. Cover the pastry with baking parchment and place ceramic baking beans on top to keep the pastry level and prevent it rising too much.

Bake in a moderately hot oven at 200°C (Conventional Electric Oven) for 17-20 minutes until lightly golden brown. Cool in the dish. Once the pastry has cooled make the custard.

To make the custard mix together the sugar, custard powder and a little milk in a 1 pint measuring jug until smooth. Add the rest of the milk and stir. Pour into a small, medium based saucepan. Gently stir the mixture, constantly, over a low to medium heat until it has thickened. Leave the custard to cool to room temperature.

To finish the flan place one layer of strawberries into the base of the flan, setting aside some strawberries for the decoration. Pour the custard over the strawberries.

Cool in the fridge for 4 – 5 hours until the custard is set and the flan is cold.

Decorate with the rest of strawberries which had been reserved for decoration and serve cold.

Apple Crumble

This dessert is delicious served warm with custard or vanilla ice cream. It is best eaten warm on the day of making, but you can refrigerate it and eat it the next day. You can make different fruit fillings for the crumble, for example apple & blueberry, apple & raspberry and a black cherry crumble, all of which work well.

Recipe Facts

Preparation Time: 25 minutes   Cooking Time: **20 minutes**

Dairy Free	Yes	**Gluten Free**	No
Egg Free	Yes	**Soya Free**	Yes
Nut Free	Yes	**Wheat Free**	No

Suitable for Freezing: **No**

Ingredients

For the apple filling:
500g sliced Bramley cooking apples
35g (approx) granulated sugar
A little cold water

For the crumble topping:
250g plain flour, sifted
90g demerara sugar
125g non-dairy sunflower margarine

Method

To make the apple filling place the sliced apples into a bowl that is suitable to go into the microwave. Sprinkle the sugar over the apples and then pour over a little cold water so that the base of the bowl is just about covered with water. The water helps the apples to cook. Stir the apples.

Cook the apples for about 7 minutes in a microwave, stirring the apples at 2-3 minute intervals. I used a 900W microwave grade E, so you might want to cook it for slightly less or slightly longer depending on the type of microwave you may have.

Once the apples are stewed, taste them as they might need some more sugar depending on how sweet you like your desserts and how sour the apples are.
Cool the apples in the dish to room temperature.

Please note that if you do not have a microwave you can stew the apples in a pan. The same method applies but the cooking time might vary slightly. You will need to stew the apples in a medium based saucepan over a low heat, stirring occasionally so the apples do not stick to the bottom of the pan, until the apples are cooked. This may take about 8–10 minutes, but the time may vary. Taste the apples to see if they need any more sugar. Cool in the pan to room temperature.

To make the crumble topping add the flour and sugar into a large mixing bowl and mix together.

Rub in the margarine with your hands until the mixture resembles fine breadcrumbs. Into a round ovenproof casserole dish, place the stewed apples.

Sprinkle the crumble topping over the apples.

Bake in a moderate oven at 180°C (160 – 170 °C) (Conventional Electric Oven) for about 20-22 minutes, or until lightly golden brown.

Serve warm with custard or non-dairy vanilla ice cream if preferred.

Chocolate Pie

This is a great summer dessert for chocoholics! The cold, crisp pastry works really well with the rich, soft chocolate filling to make a delicious and light dessert. Instead of decorating it with walnuts you could use flaked almonds, which are equally as tasty. I prefer using chilled pastry instead of frozen as the texture and taste is better and it's easier to roll out.

Recipe Facts

Preparation Time: **40 minutes**   Cooking Time: **25 minutes**

Dairy Free	Yes		**Gluten Free**	No
Egg Free	Yes		**Soya Free**	No
Nut Free	Optional		**Wheat Free**	No

Suitable for Freezing: **No**

Ingredients

330g ready made non-dairy short crust pastry
30g cornflour
2 tbsp cocoa powder, sifted
2 tbsp decaffeinated cold coffee
4 tbsp soya milk & 450ml soya milk extra
30g non-dairy sunflower margarine
5 tbsp granulated sugar
10 walnut halves (optional)

Method

Grease a round fluted flan dish (23cm in diameter).

Roll out the pastry on a lightly floured board until it is large enough to cover the base and sides of the dish (approx 29cm in diameter). Then carefully line the dish with the pastry. Prick the pastry a few times with a fork, this is to let the air out when it is cooking.

Cover the pastry with some baking parchment and place some ceramic baking beans in the dish. This is to keep the pastry level when it is cooking and to stop it rising too much.

Bake in a moderately hot oven at 200°C (Conventional Electric Oven) for 12 minutes, take it out of the oven and carefully remove the baking beans and paper. Place the pastry back into the oven and cook for a further 3-5 minutes or until the pastry is cooked and is lightly golden brown. Cool to room temperature.

To make the chocolate mousse blend together the cornflour, cocoa and cold coffee with 4 tbsp soya milk in a 1 pint jug until it is a smooth paste. Pour ¾ pint of soya milk into a medium based saucepan and bring to the boil.

Take the pan off the heat and whisk in the smooth paste until thoroughly combined. Return the pan to the heat and bring to the boil, stirring continuously.

Once it has come to the boil add the margarine and sugar and beat the mixture with a hand whisk for about 2 minutes.

To make the pie pour the moose mixture immediately into the prepared pastry case. Cool to room temperature then refrigerate until it has set and is completely cold.

Decorate with 10 walnut halves (optional).

Rich Chocolate Pudding

This pudding has both a sponge base and a sauce which I think makes it an extra special dessert. If you like chocolate you will definitely like this dessert, it's a chocoholics' dream. As it is quite rich it is nice served with some non-dairy ice cream and maybe some fruit such as strawberries.

Recipe Facts

Preparation Time: 45 minutes   Cooking Time: **30 minutes**

Dairy Free	Yes	**Gluten Free**	No
Egg Free	Yes	**Soya Free**	No
Nut Free	Yes	**Wheat Free**	No

Suitable for Freezing: **No**

Ingredients

For the mixture:
125g granulated sugar
65g non-dairy sunflower margarine
190ml soya milk
140g self-raising flour, sifted
25g cocoa powder, sifted
140g plain dark chocolate (70% cocoa), chopped

For the sauce:
25g cocoa powder, sifted
250g dark muscovado sugar
250ml boiling water

Method

Grease a 2 pint pudding basin with the non-dairy sunflower margarine.

Cream together the granulated sugar and margarine in a large mixing bowl until light and fluffy.

Add the milk and stir well. You may want to use an electric hand blender to combine the three ingredients together. Do not worry if the mixture looks like it has curdled.

Add the flour and cocoa powder and mix well until combined. You may want to use an electric hand blender to make sure there are no lumps of flour remaining.

Add the chocolate and stir well.

Spoon the mixture into the prepared pudding basin.

For the sauce add the cocoa powder and muscovado sugar into a small bowl and mix well. Add the boiling water and stir well until all the sugar has dissolved.

Gently pour the sauce over the sponge mixture, making sure it does not splash.

Bake in a moderate oven at 180°C (Conventional Electric Oven) for about 30-35 minutes or until the sponge is springy to touch.

Serve warm with non-dairy vanilla ice cream and maybe some fresh strawberries if desired.

Sticky Toffee Pudding

This gooey, toffee pudding is an English classic and just as popular as ever. There is a slight twist to the making of this pudding as the sponge mixture and sauce cook in the basin at the same time, so you don't have to make the sauce separately which I find is a great time saver. Goes very well with some non-dairy vanilla ice cream.

Recipe Facts

Preparation Time: **45 minutes**   Cooking Time: **40 minutes**

Dairy Free	Yes	**Gluten Free**	No
Egg Free	Yes	**Soya Free**	No
Nut Free	Yes	**Wheat Free**	No

Suitable for Freezing: **No**

Ingredients

For the sponge mixture:
175g self-raising flour, sifted
100g dark muscovado sugar
125ml soya milk
50g non-dairy sunflower margarine
1tsp vanilla extract
200g rolled dates, chopped

For the sauce:
200g dark muscovado sugar
25g non-dairy sunflower margarine, diced
500ml boiling water

Method

Grease a 2 pint pudding basin with non-dairy sunflower margarine.

Put the sifted flour and the dark muscovado sugar into a large mixing bowl and stir well.

Combine the milk, melted margarine and vanilla extract in a 1 pint glass jug. Add this carefully to the dry ingredients and mix well. You may want to use an electric blender to make sure there are no lumps of flour remaining in the mixture.

Add the dates and mix well.

To make the sauce for the pudding sprinkle the dark muscovado sugar over the pudding mixture. Carefully place the diced margarine cubes over the top of the sugar so they are evenly distributed. Gently pour the boiling water over the sugar and margarine taking care not to let it splash.

Bake in a moderate oven at 190°C (Conventional Electric Oven) for about 40-45 minutes or until it is springy to touch.

Serve warm with non-dairy ice cream.

Apple Pie

An old fashioned favourite. This pie is delicious served warm or cold with custard and makes a great dessert. You can make various fruit fillings for the pie, for example my Grandma used to make a fabulous blackcurrant pie. Apple & blackberry, plum or rhubarb also make excellent alternatives.

Recipe Facts

Preparation Time: **45 minutes**   Cooking Time: **35 minutes**

Dairy Free	Yes	**Gluten Free**	No
Egg Free	Yes	**Soya Free**	No
Nut Free	Yes	**Wheat Free**	No

Suitable for Freezing: **Yes**

Ingredients

For the apple filling:
400g sliced Bramley cooking apples
30g granulated sugar
A little cold water

For the pastry:
500g non-dairy short crust pastry
A sprinkling of demerara sugar
A little cold water

Method

To make the apple filling place the sliced apples into a bowl that is suitable to go into the microwave. Sprinkle the sugar over the apples and then pour over a little cold water so that the base of the bowl is just about covered with water. The water helps the apples to cook. Stir the apples.

Cook the apples for about 6 minutes in a microwave, stirring the apples at 2-3 minute intervals. I used a 900W microwave so you might want to cook it for slightly less or slightly longer depending on the type of microwave you have.

Once the apples are stewed, taste them as they might need some more sugar depending on how sweet you like your desserts and how sour the apples are. Cool the apples in the dish to room temperature.

Please note that if you do not have a microwave you can stew the apples in a pan. The same method applies but the cooking time might vary slightly. You will need to stew the apples in a medium based saucepan over a low heat, stirring occasionally so the apples do not stick to the bottom of the pan, until the apples are cooked. This may take about 8-10 minutes, but the time may vary. Taste the apples to see if they need any more sugar. Cool in the pan to room temperature.

To make the pie grease a round glass shallow pie dish (18cm diameter for the base, 20cm diameter across the top and 2 ½ cm deep). I use the glass lid of a casserole dish.

Roll out approximately 280g of the pastry on a lightly floured board to about 25-26cm in diameter. This is going to line the sides and base of the dish.

Carefully lift the pastry off the board and place it gently into the dish.

Roll out approximately 220g of the pastry on a lightly floured board to about 22-23cm in diameter. This is going to be the top of the pie.

Spoon the stewed apples into the dish which has been lined with pastry. Level the apples out so they are evenly distributed.

Carefully place the pastry, which has been reserved for the top, over the apples. Pinch the edges of the pastry together (i.e. the bottom pastry with the top pastry) so the apples do not spill out when it is cooking.

With a pair of scissors snip the pastry three times in the centre to create holes for the air to escape whilst the pie is cooking.

Lightly brush the top of the pie with cold water and sprinkle with demerara sugar.

Bake in a moderate oven at 180°C (Conventional Electric Oven) for about 25-30 minutes or until cooked and lightly golden brown.

Serve warm or cold with custard or non-dairy vanilla ice cream if preferred.

Breads

Herb Focaccia

If you like tasty herb bread, you will like this herb focaccia. It is full of fresh herbs which is what makes it so tasty. It makes quite a large piece of bread, so it's ideal if you are having a party, or you can simply cut it up and freeze it. It's delicious toasted and served warm or on its own with some good quality olive oil.

Recipe Facts

Preparation Time: **45 mins + 2 hours to rise**   Cooking Time: **15 mins**

Dairy Free	Yes	Gluten Free	No
Egg Free	Yes	Soya Free	Yes
Nut Free	Yes	Wheat Free	No

Suitable for Freezing: **Yes**

Ingredients

500g strong white bread flour, sifted
1 rounded tsp salt
1 sachet (7g) easy blend dried yeast
A handful of fresh curly parsley, chopped
A handful of fresh flat leaf parsley, chopped
A handful of fresh basil, chopped
A small bunch of fresh chives, chopped
1 tsp fresh rosemary, finely chopped
300ml hand-hot water
3 tbsp extra virgin olive oil

Method

Line a large oven tray with kitchen foil. Grease it and sprinkle with flour. Shake off any excess flour.

Into a large mixing bowl, add flour, salt, yeast and all the fresh herbs and mix well.

Make a well in the centre and add the water and oil. Mix well to form a dough.

Turn the dough out onto a lightly floured surface. Knead the dough for about 5 minutes until the dough is smooth and elastic.

Place the dough onto the prepared oven tray and press into a round about 25cm (10 inches) in diameter.

Cover the dough with a clean tea towel and leave in a warm place for about 2 hours or until it has approximately doubled in size.

Cook in a hot oven at 220°C (Conventional Electric Oven) for 10 minutes then cook for a further 5-10 minutes in a moderately hot oven at 200°C (Conventional Electric Oven) until lightly golden and it should sound hollow when gently tapped.

Cool on the tray.

Breakfast Buns

These breakfast buns make an excellent start to the day. Soft in texture and packed full of fruit they are perfect toasted and served with a cup of tea or coffee. They do take a long time to make as you need to let the dough rise, but they are definitely worth the wait.

Recipe Facts

Preparation Time: **45 mins + 2 hours to rise** **Cooking Time:** **15 mins**

Dairy Free	Yes	**Gluten Free**	No
Egg Free	Yes	**Soya Free**	No
Nut Free	Yes	**Wheat Free**	No

Suitable for Freezing: **Yes**

Ingredients

250g strong white bread flour, sifted
250g plain flour, sifted
¼ tsp salt
2 rounded tsp cinnamon
1 whole nutmeg, grated
1 sachet (7g) of 'easy to use' dried yeast
90g dried sour cherries, roughly chopped
30g dried apricots, chopped
30g mixed candied peel
45ml (3 tbsp) soya milk and 45ml (3 tbsp) hot water, mixed together
60ml (4 tbsp) soya milk and 100ml hot and cold water, mixed together
90g non-dairy sunflower margarine, melted
90g granulated sugar

Method

Line an ovenproof tray (25cm by 40cm) with kitchen foil. Grease the foil and sprinkle with flour. Shake off the excess flour that does not stick to the foil.

Into a large bowl, add the sifted fours, salt, spices, yeast, dried fruit and mixed peel and mix together. Make a well in the centre.

Put 3 tbsp of soya milk and 3 tbsp of boiling hot water into a teacup and stir.

Add 4 tbsp of soya milk into a 1pt measuring jug and make up to 150ml with a mixture of cold and boiling hot water until the liquid is at a hand hot temperature. To this liquid mixture, immediately add the milk/water mixture from the teacup, melted margarine and sugar. Stir until the sugar has dissolved a little.

Pour the liquid mixture into the dry ingredients. Using your hands, mix to form a dough.

Turn the dough out onto a lightly floured surface and knead for about 5 minutes until smooth and elastic.

Divide the dough into 15 equal round portions and place onto the prepared oven tray. Cover the dough with a tea towel and place it in a warm place for about 2 hours until doubled in size.

Remove the tea towel and bake in a moderately hot oven at 200°C (Conventional Electric Oven) for about 15-17 minutes until the buns are golden brown in colour.

Whilst still hot, brush the buns with soya milk and sprinkle with sugar.

Cool on the trays.

Sauces, Icings & Fillings

Plain Butter Cream

Ingredients

155g non-dairy sunflower margarine
90g icing sugar, sifted

Method

Into a small bowl, add the margarine and sugar and mix until smooth and creamy.

Lemon Butter Cream

Ingredients

Grated rind of 2 lemons
155g non-dairy sunflower margarine
90g icing sugar, sifted

Method

Take a small bowl and add the rind, margarine and sugar. Mix until smooth and creamy.

Chocolate Butter Cream

Ingredients

155g non-dairy sunflower margarine
105g icing sugar, sifted
60g cocoa powder, sifted

Method

Into a small bowl, add the margarine and sugar and mix until smooth and creamy.

Add the cocoa powder and stir well.

Banana Cream

Ingredients

155g non-dairy sunflower margarine
90g icing sugar, sifted
185g bananas, chopped

Method

Into a small bowl add the margarine and sugar. Mix until smooth and creamy.

Add the banana and mix well.

Lemon Icing

Ingredients

Grated rind of 1 lemon
Juice of half a lemon
Icing sugar, sifted

Method

Into a small bowl add the rind and lemon juice. Mix in enough icing sugar to make it to the right consistency to spread.

Passion Fruit Icing

Ingredients

Pulp of 2 small passion fruits
Icing sugar, sifted

Method

Spoon out the pulp of two passion fruits into a small bowl.

Add enough icing sugar to make it to the right consistency.

Chocolate Icing

Ingredients

125g icing sugar, sifted
60ml cold water (approx)
55g cocoa powder, sifted

Method

Into a small bowl add the icing sugar and a little water and stir until the icing sugar has dissolved.

Add the cocoa powder and stir until smooth and there are no lumps

Plain White Icing

Ingredients

75g icing sugar, sifted
30ml cold water (approx)

Method

Into a small bowl add the icing sugar and a little water and stir until the icing sugar has dissolved and it's the right consistency to spread.

Rum Sauce

Ingredients

2tbsp granulated sugar
2 tbsp cornflour
600ml soya milk
15-30ml (1-2 tbsp) dark rum

Method

Into a 1 pint measuring jug mix together the sugar, cornflour and a little milk until smooth.

Add the rest of the remaining milk and stir.

Pour into a small, medium based saucepan. Stir the mixture constantly over a medium heat until it has thickened.

Add the rum and stir.

Serve immediately.

Orange Icing

Ingredients

185g icing sugar, sifted
Grated rind of 1 large orange
30ml orange juice (approx)

Method

Add the rind and icing sugar into a small bowl. Stir well.

Gradually add the orange juice, stirring well after each addition.

Custard

Ingredients

2 level tbsp granulated sugar
2 rounded tbsp custard powder
600ml soya milk

Method

Mix together the sugar, custard powder and a little milk in a 1 pint measuring jug until it has gone smooth.

Add the rest of the milk and stir.

Pour into a small, medium based saucepan. Stir the mixture constantly over a medium heat until it has thickened. Serve immediately.

Conversion Charts

Temperature

Circotherm	Conventional Electric		Gas Mark
°C	°F	°C	
100	200	100	1/4
110	225	110	1/4
120	250	130	1/2
130	275	140	1
140	300	150	2
150	325	160	3
160	350-375	180-190	4-5
170	400	200	6
180	425	220	7
190	450-500	230	8-9

Dry Measurements

Metric	Imperial
15g	1/2 oz
30g	1oz
60g	2oz
90g	3oz
125g	4oz (1/2 lb)
155g	5oz
185g	6oz
220g	7oz
250g	8oz (1/2 lb)
280g	9oz
315g	10oz
345g	11oz
375g	12oz (3/4 lb)
410g	13oz
440g	14oz
470g	15oz
500g	16oz (1lb)
750g	24oz (1 1/2 lb)
1kg	32oz (2 lb)

Liquid Measurements

Metric	Imperial
30ml	1 fluid oz
60ml	2 fluid oz
100ml	3 fluid oz
125ml	4 fluid oz
150ml	5 fluid oz (1/4 pint)
190ml	6 fluid oz
250ml	8 fluid oz
300ml	10 fluid oz (1/2 pint)
500ml	16 fluid oz
600ml	20 fluid oz (1 pint)
1000ml (1 litre)	1 3/4 pints

Baking Tin Measurements

Metric	Imperial
3mm	1/8inch
6mm	1/4inch
1cm	1/2inch
2cm	3/4inch
2.5cm	1inch
5cm	2inch
6cm	2 1/2inch
8cm	3inch
10cm	4inch
13cm	5inch
15cm	6inch
18cm	7inch
20cm	8inch
23cm	9inch
25cm	10inch
28cm	11inch
30cm	12inch

Index of Recipes